Education for Rural Development

(Strictly on the Basis of Prescribed Syllabus with Modern Trends)

Education for Rural Development

(Strictly on the Basis of Prescribed Syllabus with Modern Trends)

Tushar K Sinha

AUTHORSPRESS

Worldwide Circulation through Authorspress Global Network
First Published 2009
by
Authorspress
E-35/103, Jawahar Park
Laxmi Nagar, Delhi-110 092
e-mail: authorspress@yahoo.com

Education for Rural Development
ISBN 978-81-7273-493-0

Printed in India at Tarun Offset, Delhi.

Preface

In the fifty years since Independence, India has advanced technologically to become a major force in the global market. All this could not be possible without the spread of education to every level. Though the urban centres have become highly advanced, the rural grass root level still lags behind, and for power to reach the people, they must become educationally self sufficient. Education has been by and large agreed upon by all societies and civilizations as the major mode of spreading development within the social realm, and conjoined with the rural context, education is one of the most potent weapons for development within India, since its rural heartland is where India's majority of a population resides, and any talk of development is incomplete without regard to the rural scenario.

The present text has been designed as a manual which looks into field of rural development and education with a view to enhance the reader's understanding of the educational practices and schemes which have been undertaken by governments in India in the post-Independence scenario to be spread education and further development. It seeks to enhance the reader's comprehension of the field of rural development in a panoramic manner, looking into the current problems and issues which surround the field, as well as enabling insight into the proper development of the field further. The critical comments of experts should particularly prove to be of immense help to the readers.

It is hoped that the insight and erudition of the text serves well for all. Any suggestions for further improvement are most welcome.

Tushar K Sinha

Contents

1

Transforming Rural Areas

Rural areas are generally open areas, with low settled population densities. A high proportion of the unsettled land area and/or land used is for primary production (mining, agriculture, livestock, forestry, fisheries). The residents of rural areas are largely dependent—either directly or indirectly—on these primary production activities as their principal, if not their only, source of livelihood.

Studies estimated that for the next two decades, the majority of the population living in developing countries will continue to be rural. This is even more the case for the least developed countries where the people living in rural areas will still represent over 55 per cent of the total population in 2030. In other words, during this period, the development challenge will continue to be related to rural trends and conditions.

Consequently achieving the targets set by the World Food Summit for the year 2015 will require particular emphasis on rural areas. In spite of this fact, the decreasing attention being paid to rural issues is probably due to a large extent to global demographic trends and the focus on urbanisation and its implications on development. Indeed, the twentieth century witnessed an important redistribution of the world's population towards urban areas.

Whereas 66 per cent of human beings lived in rural areas in 1960, by 2000 that proportion had declined to 53 per cent, which however, still constitutes the majority of the world population. Furthermore, most recent projections suggest that the rural population of the less developed regions will increase very slowly until 2025. As from this period, the rural population of the less developed regions is expected to start declining, following the trend experienced by more developed regions since 1950. Except for Africa and Oceania, the rural population is expected to decline in all areas between 2000 and 2030.

In spite of these global trends confirming the urbanisation scenario, available data also document the strength of rurality. It is worth noting that the bulk of the rural population is concentrated in a few countries, 35 nations representing 85 per cent of the world rural population in 2000. In 2030, it is expected that Bangladesh, Pakistan and Indonesia will join China and India in the group of countries recording over 100 million people living in rural areas.

1.1. Poverty

Poverty has recently re-emerged as the focus of development efforts at the international level. For the international community, poverty is now considered as the greatest challenge. Of special concern are the 1.2 billion people living on less than $1 a day and the additional 1.6 billion living on less than $2 a day. Poverty reduction efforts take place within a broader development framework agreed upon at the Millennium summit held in New York in September 2000. One could expect that such an agenda, including the mobilisation against poverty, leads to greater attention paid to rural issues. Indeed, in developing countries rurality often equates to poverty. Yet, in spite of significant rural-urban migration, the great majority of the poor are still rural. Average income levels remain lower in the countryside than in cities and a larger share of the population is living below specified poverty lines. It is estimated that 1.2 billion people live in extreme poverty, meaning that they spend less than a 'standard' dollar a day. Among them about 75 per cent live in rural areas.

Furthermore, despite urbanisation, 60 per cent of the world poor are still expected to be rural people by 2020. To a large extent, reducing poverty requires first addressing the challenge of rural poverty. Moreover, the development situation of rural communities differ considerably within one country according to the degree of access to vital services (roads, marketing facilities, administration, schools, health stations). Well served rural areas are better off than neglected urban slum settlements. This has serious effects on the quality of basic education and the opportunities for development.

The regional distribution of poverty has not changed much over the past decade. It is of course very much related to the relative size of the population in the different regions of the developing world. South Asia remains the region with the largest number of poor and their absolute number has increased marginally in spite of recorded GDP growth. On the contrary, in East Asia, the second largest location by the absolute number of poor, poverty declined significantly due to the economic progress recorded in China. The situation continues to deteriorate in sub-Saharan Africa where the number of poor has been growing due to stagnation of per capita incomes. Africa is the region with the largest share of people living in poverty.

Landless farm workers and casually employed farm labourers often form the majority of the poor in rural areas. However, in Africa, smallholders constitute the largest category of poor. Beyond the occupational dimension, children everywhere are more affected by poverty than adults. In many countries the poverty incidence among women is higher than among men.

Notably, the new International Bank for Reconstruction and Development/International Development Association (IBRD/IDA) strategy for rural development aims specifically at reaching the rural poor. Putting poverty in a broader conceptual framework also constitutes a feature of more recent approaches.

Within a sustainable livelihood framework, reducing poverty does not only involve better income, it also concerns providing broader livelihood-related choices. Expanding livelihood choices involves placing greater emphasis on the interface between agriculture production and other activities. Emerging forms of diversified livelihoods contribute to spreading risk and reducing vulnerability.

Vulnerability of the poor restricts their livelihood choices. In many countries vulnerability has increased recently as a result of a growing prevalence of HIV/AIDS and political disturbance. Poverty-reduction efforts, particularly in rural areas, involve reducing poor people's vulnerability.

Recognising the assets and diverse strategies of poor households, the livelihoods approach tends to question the classical farm-based orthodoxy of rural poverty reduction. While rural livelihood strategies potentially renew inspiration for conceiving poverty-reduction strategies, their practical implications need to be further articulated. Thus, the debate on the contribution of agricultural growth to poverty reduction is far from closed. Recent empirical evidence confirms the poverty-alleviating effects of agricultural growth. While recognising the value of other development efforts, some authors consider that agriculture development remains the most powerful instrument to reduce rural poverty.

The continued neglect of rural development priorities can also lead to a host of other problems that can undermine achievement of national development goals. Such problems include illiteracy, the spread of HIV/ AIDS and other endemic diseases, as well as increased 'pushed-out' migration to urban areas. In turn, this may lead to growth of slums, rising informal underemployment, breakdown of the family, rising social alienation, increased crime (including drug-related crime), increased wealth disparities, political alienation and organised anti-state violence and hence, a need for increased police protection, increased costs of controlling pollution, sanitation, health and so on.

1.2. Food Security and Globalisation

In spite of the progress made in agricultural production, restricted access to food and inadequate nutrition remain the most visible and severe form of poverty. Hence, under-nutrition and food insecurity persist in many parts of the world. The 1996 World Food Summit in Rome reaffirmed "the right of everyone to have access to safe and nutritious food, consistent with the right to adequate food and the fundamental right of everyone to be free from hunger"

Today, although enough food is being produced for everyone on earth to be adequately nourished, unfortunately food security is not truly guaranteed—in quantity or quality—anywhere in the world. In many low income countries, food production capacities are deteriorating as a result of soil erosion, water shortages and demographics. However, the present pattern of food security shows that resource distribution is a central issue at both the national and international levels. The persistence of hunger is largely due to our inability to spread the increase in agricultural yields more widely and to ensure that available resources are distributed.

There have also been major transformations in the modes of production and consumption of agricultural products, and particularly food products. The liberalisation of national economies and world trade has fundamentally changed the problem of access to foodstuffs and to land:

- liberalisation leads to a situation in which the equilibrium between food supply and demand is no longer sought through self-sufficiency policies, but through increased trade between countries having a food surplus and countries having a food deficit;
- it also leads to the abandonment of agrarian reform policies in favour of giving encouragement to private farms that are fully integrated into the market economy.

1.3. Education in Rural Areas

Education in rural areas is closely related to the broader rural development concept. Like education for rural people, rural development has been a very productive field in development studies. In the 1960s, the Green Revolution reflected a vision of rural development associated with large scale monocrop farming supported by massive state investment. As in education in the 1970s, a significant discourse on the transformation of rural areas and agrarian reform found its inspiration in Marxist theories. In a schematic view, the 1960s could be seen as the period of modernisation, the 1970s as the era of state intervention, the 1980s as market liberalisation and structural adjustment while the late 1990s stressed concepts and approaches such as empowerment and sustainable livelihoods in a broader context of poverty reduction strategy.

Today, both domains are now recognising similar intervention principles, including:

- focusing on poverty reduction;
- recognising the potential of indigenous knowledge;
- promoting the use of participatory approaches;

- emphasising community involvement;
- coping with state retreat within the context of structural adjustment programmes and liberalisation policies;
- adopting an holistic view of the development of the rural space;
- preparing rural people for off-farm employment by building knowledge and skills capacity;
- understanding the complementarity of urban/rural linkages;
- developing partnerships with NGOs and the civil society;
- focusing on gender issues; and
- focusing on HIV/AIDS issues.

Such parallelism between these two spheres of development thinking and practice suggests that they have much to learn one from another. Besides recognising the symbiotic nature of rural development and education, it seems important to underline the current transformation of development thinking and its implications for education in rural areas. To a large extent, for about two decades, development policies have been shaped by two approaches to development which reflected contradictions within the UN system.

Action to promote basic education in rural areas involves:

- targeting multiple stakeholders, focusing on 'Education for All' in harmony with the renewed commitment made by the international community at the World Education Forum held in Dakar, 2000 and on 'Food for All' as stated at the World Food Summit;
- contributing to placing education at the core of the global and national development agenda and food security agenda, by focusing on the following priorities:
  - expanding access to education and improving school attendance in rural areas;
  - improving the quality of education;
  - finding appropriate ways to incorporate rural development and food security in the basic education curriculum.

– strengthening institutional capacity in planning and managing education for rural development and food security.

In most countries public policies fail to combine and integrate rural development and basic education. This is often due to the division of responsibility at national level, with usually one ministry having responsibility for education, especially the formal education sector, and perhaps several other ministries addressing their own remits. Many donors have to work through a particular ministry, and hence donor support tends to be fractionated as well. This is a common and rather depressing picture in terms of the impact of interventions, with efforts dissipated and a lack of co-ordination on the ground where grassroots movements need support. Providing a strong conceptual framework within which support to rural development and basic education can be located should contribute to increased overall policy effectiveness.

1.4. Contribution of Education to Rural Development

1.4.1. Agriculture and Economic Growth

The development theoreticians of the 1960s viewed agricultural growth as the principal force driving a nation's development. For example, Arthur Lewis wrote in 1954, "if agriculture is in a slump, it offers only a stagnant market and hampers the development of the rest of the economy. If agricultural development is neglected, it becomes more difficult to develop anything else: this is the fundamental principle of balanced growth".

The idea that agriculture plays an important role in the overall economic growth of developing countries seems to be confirmed by the existence of a correlation between increased agricultural yields and increases in total output. Of the 68 countries for which we have reliable data, 30 saw their agricultural production increase by over 3 per cent annually during the 1970s and 1980s. In all of these countries, the average GDP growth rate was at least 2.5 per cent during the period, and twothirds of the countries with strong growth of agricultural output also recorded very high rates of economic growth.

1.4.2. Human Capital Theory

According to human capital theory, the educational level of the agricultural labour force has an influence on agricultural productivity. This relationship may take three forms:

- education can improve the quality of farmers' labour by enabling them to produce more with their available stock of production factors (other than labour);
- education can increase the efficiency of resource allocation;
- education can help farmers to choose more effective means of production by adopting new techniques.

1.4.3. Need New Educational Policies

In the 1960s and 1970s, the numerous debates over the role played by education in the growth of agricultural output led to the adoption of a set of reforms in educational systems. The main objective of these reforms was to bring schools closer to the rural world not only by instruction in agricultural techniques but also by the use of new teaching methods. These policies have often been referred to collectively as 'ruralisation', but this is in fact a term that recalls certain practices used under the colonial regime.

During the colonial period, ruralisation of education was one of the two facets of the colonial strategy: (i) humanistic education to prepare the elites and the staff of the colonial administration; (ii) a second track of practically-oriented education for the rural population. In the post-independence context, this concept does not reflect the complexity of the efforts to adopt an educational approach that ensures the relevance of education to its environment without the discriminatory purpose explicit in the colonial 'ruralisation' strategies.

A first approach attempted to adapt primary education to the specific conditions of life in rural communities by changing programmes and content. The purpose of this strategy was to better integrate schools into the rural environment by developing knowledge and practical skills in line with the requirements of the population and by preserving local values.

Summarising these efforts, the 1982 Conference of Ministers of Education and Ministers responsible for Economic Planning of the Member States of Africa stated that, "educational policies since the late 1960s reflect a concern with putting education, at all levels, at the service of agricultural and rural development. It must be given a 'rural' orientation to encourage more pupils to pursue agricultural activities, in order to foster the development of rural areas and as a result to curb migration to the cities".

1.4.4. Making Schools Relevant to the Rural Environment

The reforms and projects implemented to adapt primary education to the specific needs of the rural population aimed to provide functional education and training in order to give children a better knowledge of their environment and to teach them the farming trade. The objectives of these programmes were both economic and social. More generally, many developing countries tried to adapt schools to the rural environment and to agricultural activities. Some of the measures taken to improve the relevance of education were, for instance:

1.4.4.1. Productive work in schools

Curricular reforms were aimed at making primary education more relevant, for example by introducing manual activities in rural schools. Certain countries introduced practical subjects to promote the acquisition of occupational skills that could subsequently be used on the labour market. For example, the educational reform undertaken by Rwanda in 1979 aimed to integrate productive work into all levels of primary education. Practical subjects constituted the core of the education provided. The main objective of this type of reform was to integrate primary school pupils into the rural productive process, familiarising them with agricultural activities in order to enable them—with their parents—to develop the resources available in their environment in an optimal manner.

Cuban experience in school gardening was and still is famous all over the world and inspired several other countries. In Burkina Faso, the concern for taking the real economic conditions of the country into account in education and training activities led the authorities to set up a system of rural schools as early as the 1960s. Rural schools were supposed to teach young people who had passed the age for entry into primary school to read and write and to train them in new agricultural methods. The goal was to train modern farmers capable of introducing the changes needed for development.

In Zambia, the education system reform of 1977 consisted of introducing 'production units' in rural schools, with the objective of providing skills corresponding to the needs of the economy, notably for pupils who had left the formal educational system. This reform was thus supposed to allow pupils to learn production techniques and to promote the spirit and practice of self-sufficiency.

This educational philosophy was in many cases accompanied by an objective of making schools self-financing. Some, such as Benin and Senegal, sought to create 'school co-operatives' capable of generating income. Later on, productive work at school and the creation of school cooperatives came to be seen as stopgap measures in a context of shrinking budgets and structural adjustment.

School gardens

The use of school gardens was, and to a certain extent still is, a very widespread practice in developing countries. Gardens are used as teaching tools where pupils can put into practice what they have learned. They serve as a means of teaching and learning about farming techniques and of introducing new seed varieties or new and improved technologies. In addition, gardens were seen as a way to provide food to school canteens. In the poorest rural areas, this contribution was also considered as an important source of nutritional supplement for children who do not always receive regular meals. Finally, school gardens were also used to promote respect for manual work, linkages with the community and to teach life skills and ideology.

1.4.4.2. Community schools

The main idea behind community schools was that "the school should occupy a central position within the village in order to put itself fully at the service of the community; and the education of children should be linked to that of adults". In this perspective, the content of school programmes should be based on the real needs of the community. Primary education was to be "practical, utilitarian and pragmatic". The idea was to integrate the school into the surrounding community by establishing a two-way relationship: pupils participate in work in the fields, in road construction, etc. and parents become familiar with school activities as part of a large-scale literacy programme.

1.4.4.3. Languages of instruction

Considering that the mother tongue is the best vehicle for teaching, the 1976 Lagos Conference of Education Ministers strongly reaffirmed the importance of using African languages as the languages of instruction during the first years of primary schooling.

1.4.4.4. School mapping, school calendar and the pace of education

Another strategy for broadening access to primary education in rural areas was to introduce more flexibility in the way schools function. This was done by establishing new primary education structures that were more flexible than the traditional norms and framework. Resorting to multilevel classes, for example, makes it possible to bring provision to areas of low population density.

In the rural environment, the so-called 'double-shift' system—giving a teacher two groups of pupils, one in the morning and the other in the afternoon—allows pupils to continue to participate in household economic activities. This reduces the opportunity cost of sending children to school and thus helps to improve retention rates. Along the same lines, flexible school hours were frequently introduced in rural areas in order to make the school schedule correspond to the daily and seasonal cycles of agricultural production.

The various educational measures implemented to make education more relevant to rural concerns are complementary in most cases. Such measures constitute a multidimensional approach that is as much economic and social as educational. However, these efforts have often run afoul of the many difficulties stemming from the paucity of resources available to governments for the creation of diversified programmes and appropriate teaching aids and for the provision of schoolbooks. Additional problems arose in relation to the establishment of adequate teacher training programmes.

In some schools, agricultural equipment was left unused, while in others it was lacking. Furthermore, some of these programmes met with hostility from parents, who did not see the point of having their children acquire practical knowledge which they could provide themselves.

For families, the decision to send children to school meant enabling them to acquire new knowledge in order to escape from working in the fields and to gain access to wageearning employment in the cities.

This criticism by parents reveals the complexity of the situation, because some studies show, to the contrary, that families did not send their children to school because they were worried that a school irrelevant to their environment would have alienated their children from the family and from the rural environment. In addition, some parents consider it important that schooling should not completely separate their children from their environment.

Slow progress in increasing school enrolments in remote rural areas and the debate over the irrelevance of schooling to the rural environment contributed to the emergence of non-formal education as a valid educational strategy to support, complement or sometimes even substitute the formal system.

1.4.4.5. Non-formal Education

This minimum level of education varies from one group of individuals to another and it refers to the acquisition of knowledge and know-how in complementary fields such as food, nutrition, hygiene, health, family planning, etc. By extension, perceptions of the relationships between education and rural development are broadened through the acquisition of knowledge and of functional capacities that are useful for family life and necessary for the improvement of living conditions.

Non-formal education is defined as "any organised and systematic educational activity situated outside of the traditional education system and aimed at providing certain types of education to specific population groups, adults as well as children". One of the objectives of non-formal education is to expand the learning opportunities of children not enrolled in the traditional school system and to meet the needs of the population more effectively. The multiplicity of forms and the flexibility of non-formal education are major assets that promote the adaptation of programmes to various rural contexts. Non-formal education projects are characterised by great diversity, in terms of teaching methods, the subjects taught, financing, objectives, target population and the qualifications of teaching staff.

There are various forms of non-formal education in the rural environment. They begin by singling out extension services, which are supposed to favour the transition from subsistence agriculture to market agriculture by disseminating new technologies. Agricultural training aims at the acquisition of specific skills and adopts a more institutional approach. Rural development thus demands an integrated approach which, in addition to facilitating access to education and to new technologies, mobilises a range of factors such as access to credit, to transportation, to health, etc.

The role which non-formal education can play as a complement to or even a substitute for the education system is all the more important because central governments have proved unable to meet the growing need for schooling and because rural dwellers often have little or no chance of continuing their education at the secondary level, either general or technical. The diversity of non-formal educational projects makes it difficult to arrive at an overall evaluation of their role in agricultural development. However, the first generation of experiments of this type provided many lessons as to what should be done, or not done, to capitalise on the potential existing in the rural environment in order to improve access to education for all.

The use of technology, especially radio and television, as a means of accelerating the process of instruction and literacy training spread widely in the 1950s and 1960s in developing countries. These new technologies were introduced in learning situations in an attempt to break with the traditional 'face-to-face' mode of instruction, which has a high cost. The use of radio saw tremendous expansion, as radio is a mass medium that is well known to rural communities.

The results were not always up to expectations, however, notably owing to a tendency to neglect the real concerns of farmers. In addition, all developing countries organised massive literacy campaigns. Literacy training was claimed to be "a fundamental right of every human being" and an instrument of socio-economic development.

In simplistic terms, non-formal education may be regarded as having been subject to two main criticisms, relating to its marginal status with respect to the formal education system and to its low social status. For example, most children enrolled in non-formal schools have no possibility of returning to the formal school system. In addition, the non-formal curriculum generally does not lead to a diploma that affords access to the labour market. For these reasons, in many cases people turn to non-formal education not as a result of a real choice but owing to the impossibility of gaining access to the education system.

Comparative analysis of the cost-effectiveness of formal and nonformal education projects proves difficult because of their differences of content, target audience, learning objectives, organisation, etc. Although in theory non-formal educational structures are supposed to have relatively low costs, in reality, many of them are poorly designed and proved to have low cost-effectiveness.

Over the last ten years or so, the global environment has been undergoing a radical transformation, with in particular the expansion of the market economy and the growing interdependence of countries and policies in the context of globalisation.

References

Ahmed, M.; Coombs, P.H., *Education for rural development – case studies for planners,* New York: Praeger Publishers, 1975.

Berstecher, D., *Education and rural development: issues for planning and research,* Paris: IIEP-UNESCO, 1985.

Coombs, P.H.; Manzoor, A., *Attacking rural poverty: how nonformal education can help,* Baltimore, MD: Johns Hopkins University Press, 1974.

Khan Mahmood, H., *Rural poverty in developing countries, implications for public policy.* Washington DC: International Monetary Fund, 2001.

Stiglitz, J., *Globalization and its discontents,* New York: Norton, 2002.

2

Basic Education in Rural Areas

The provision of basic education in rural areas has been heavily influenced by two main currents of development policy. The first, proper to the education sector itself, derives from the World Conference on Education for All: Meeting Basic Learning Needs. Providing basic education for all children, adolescents and adults, through formal and non-formal education, is now understood to be not only a fundamental obligation of any government that claims to respect human rights, but also to be a necessary prerequisite for social and economic development.

The commitments to Education for All undertaken at Jomtien by governments and the many development agencies present there were reinforced at several United Nations' conferences during the 1990s, beginning with the World Summit for Children. Their respective final acts underscore the important and even vital contribution that basic education for all can and must make in respect to the rights of the child, the rights of girls and women, protection of the environment, social development, food security, etc.

The second and concurrent influence on basic education in rural areas has been the world community's renewed commitments during the 1990s to alleviate poverty and give increased attention to helping the poorest in the poor countries. This has helped underscore the importance of meeting the basic learning needs of the three-quarters of the world's poor who live in rural areas. This current of development policy views basic education as a necessary and potent instrument to make improvements in various domains, such as family health, food security, employment, productivity and democratic behaviour.

Now that adult illiteracy is widely recognised to be a major obstacle to poverty alleviation, there seems to be growing awareness—not yet matched by resources—that providing basic education for adults is a necessary complement to primary schooling. Progress in providing basic education for children and for adults in rural areas can produce significant positive synergies and contribute to reducing the urban/rural gap in educational opportunity.

2.1. Primary Schooling

Rural children in low-income countries generally still have less opportunity to attend and complete primary school than do children in the better served urban areas. Countries having gross enrolment ratios (GER) approaching or exceeding 100 per cent have, in principle, the facilities to provide primary schooling for all children in the official age group if the presence of over-age children were eliminated.

Even so, the geographical distribution of schools in most developing countries is not adequate to reach all rural children. Although some rural areas lack schools altogether, another common phenomenon is the incomplete school that offers instruction in a few but not all primary grades. Children who are thus obliged to leave school at age nine or less with only two or three years of schooling have a very limited 'basic education' and are prone to losing their literacy and numeracy skills.

Even where schools exist, various economic and social obstacles prevent some children from attending them. The opportunity cost of schooling is one of the main obstacles for poor families, who would lose the income or services derived from their children's labour, either in the home or in the fields or in other work places. 'School learning' may appear quite irrelevant and unnecessary in respect to their more immediate survival needs.

Consequently, schooling must offer an attractive and affordable alternative in order for such families to accept to enrol their children in school, forego their labour and pay the direct costs of schooling, such as fees, books, materials and uniforms. In many developing countries child labour remains a considerable obstacle to EFA. Introducing more flexibility in the delivery system, particularly but not only concerning timetables, represents an important challenge to address the specific needs of working children.

Local traditions may favour boys' education and give little value, or even a negative value, to a girl's schooling. Fears that a daughter may become unmarriageable or be drawn to the city away from family surveillance need to be confronted. Parents are often worried about their daughter's safety in school and on the way to and from school. Unless such worries can be allayed, girls will continue to be unenrolled or withdrawn from school, especially as they approach puberty.

In some countries, there are also legal obstacles to schooling such as the lack of birth certificate in rural areas (e.g. Egypt) or the denial of citizenship to certain rural ethnic minorities (e.g. Thailand). Finally, war and conflicts, which affect mostly rural areas, disrupt the provision of educational services and impede access and regular attendance.

Effective access to schooling involves more than initial enrolment. Regular attendance is a minimal requirement, which unfortunately is often not met in rural schools. Health problems, malnutrition, domestic demands on children's time and seasonal demands for their labour in the fields all take their toll on attendance and therefore on learning achievement. Disrupted learning can lead to grade repetition, which in turn leads to over-age children filling primary school classes. Also, repetition is often linked to dropout. These interrelated phenomena are not unique to rural schools, but they deprive a larger proportion of rural than urban pupils from obtaining a viable basic education.

During the 1990s, two main causes of disrupted schooling, particularly in sub-Saharan Africa, were the numerous armed conflicts that have uprooted thousands of people, mainly in rural areas and the growing HIV/ AIDS pandemic that has severely reduced the number of teachers and left thousands of AIDS orphans. This situation was noted in strong terms in the African regional framework for action reported to the World Education Forum:

> The number of students dropping out of school has increased alarmingly in recent years, mainly due to increased costs or armed conflicts. Participation [school attendance] is

> particularly low amongst children in remote and rural areas, those with disabilities, refugees and internally displaced people, working children, ethnic minorities and those affected by HIV/AIDS, conflict and other emergencies that have spawned an increasing number of orphans. The poor from rural areas continue to stream into our cities where schools are already overcrowded.

Rural secondary schools are far fewer and even less well distributed than rural primary schools. Very few have hostels or other boarding arrangements, so unless families can find suitable accommodation for their child in proximity to a secondary school (an expensive and worrisome solution, especially for girls), distance selects out many potential pupils. Possibilities for distance education offer an alternative to schooling in some countries, but its potential remains largely unexploited for basic and secondary education. Apart from the occasional rural library or extension centre, other opportunities to continue self-study are still rare in rural areas.

2.1.1. Content of the Primary School Curriculum

The content of the primary school curriculum and the perception families have of it, is another important factor sometimes contributing to low enrolment and poor attendance in rural primary schools. Most developing countries have a unitary, centrally determined curriculum, which is generally designed for pupils familiar with an urban environment and may contain elements that conflict with local customs and beliefs. This 'urban bias' complicates the task of rural teachers and makes learning that much more difficult for rural children, who see little relevance of some subject matter to their own experience and to life in their community.

When school learning is perceived to be irrelevant to rural life and likely to draw children to the city, parents may see no point in sending their sons and especially their daughters to school. Yet, some efforts to 'ruralise' the curriculum have been confounded by parental objections to what they view as a sub-standard education offered to their children. However, perceptions of irrelevance can be exacerbated when the language used in school differs from the language spoken in the community or in the home.

This can also pose problems for locally recruited teachers who do not master the official language of instruction. In any case, young children obliged to learn in an unfamiliar language have an additional obstacle to overcome and are put at a great disadvantage in respect to other children learning in their mother tongue. This language constraint on learning applies more to rural communities than to urban areas, where people are more likely to have some knowledge of the country's official language even if they have another mother tongue.

2.1.2. Quality of Primary School Inputs

The quality of primary school inputs (e.g. teachers, facilities, materials) also affects school enrolment, attendance and completion rates. A good school gains parents' respect and tends to attract and retain pupils. Teachers are a key 'input', but the rural teacher is generally poorly trained, supervised, supported and remunerated. Many teachers must cope with ill-equipped classrooms overcrowded with children of several ages.

Difficult working conditions combined with a low salary that is often paid late tend to sap the morale of even dedicated teachers. Teachers of urban origin are often reluctant to take up rural assignments, and those who do accept are hard to retain in rural communities. Another serious problem in many rural communities is the frequent tardiness or absence of teachers, whether due to ill health or to other employment to make ends meet. A still more discouraging phenomenon reported by many countries is the disappearing teacher, often a victim of the HIV/AIDS pandemic.

The quality of instruction depends as well on the availability of adequate and culturally relevant textbooks, suitable writing materials for pupils, such as pencils and workbooks, as well as teaching aids, such as maps and blackboards. Very often such basic supports for learning are lacking, both in quantity and quality, in rural schools. The physical environment of the school, beginning with its proximity to the pupils' homes, also determines to a large extent the quality of schooling.

Other important physical factors include the climatic suitability of the building; the adequacy and repair of the classrooms and other facilities; ventilation and lighting; the existence and condition of a playground, a garden and toilets for the children (separate for boys and girls); and the supply of electricity and drinking water. With few exceptions, urban schools were found to be better equipped than rural schools, especially with respect to the supply of water and electricity. Also, the physical deterioration and general disrepair of school buildings in rural areas are frequently noted in inspection reports.

2.1.2.1. Home Environment

Another very important factor in the quality equation is the pupil and the home environment. Children who have had good intellectual stimulation and language training, either at home or through participation in an early childhood development (ECD) programme, are well prepared to learn in school. Unfortunately, this is not the case for many rural children. Also, as noted earlier, children coming from a home with a language other than the school language have another obstacle to overcome.

Furthermore, the fatigue experienced by children burdened with timeconsuming household chores or who must walk long distances to attend school also undermines their learning in school and at home. Children who are undernourished or otherwise in poor health have difficulty concentrating and attending class regularly. The World Food Programme describes this situation in these terms:

When poor children do go to school, they often leave home on an empty stomach. Three hundred million of the world's children are chronically hungry: the approximately 170 million of these children who attend school must learn while fighting hunger.

A study on school health and nutrition commissioned for the World Education Forum noted: "As numerous studies show, education and health are inseparable: nutritional deficiencies, helminth infections and malaria affect school participation and learning." It went on to say: "Health and nutrition status affect enrolment, retention and absenteeism". This is certainly the case in many rural schools.

2.2. Modes of Basic Education

Formal schooling is not the only vehicle of basic education found in rural areas. Some organised pre-school activities for young children contribute to their basic education and school readiness, and a variety of non-formal education and training activities provide basic learning opportunities for out-of-school children, adolescents and adults. In addition, various institutions and services (e.g. health clinics, libraries, agricultural extension) and media (e.g. radio, newspapers, folk theatre) provide rural people with useful information and support informal learning by children and adults.

Also, one should not overlook the organised learning offered through non-formal religious instruction (Koranic schools, temple schools, etc.), informal apprenticeships and traditional practices, often of a religious nature, such as story telling, initiation rites and periods of residency with monks. Finally, there are various forms of indigenous, traditional learning provided by families and by communal groups. All of these forms of learning often play an important role in rural communities and help shape people's understanding of their social and natural environment.

2.2.1. Early Childhood Development (ECD) Programmes

Early childhood development (ECD) programmes are generally more available in urban than rural areas. Cameroon reported an overall decrease in ECD gross enrolment ratios for most of its 11 provinces between 1990 and 1997; in the latter year the ratios ranged from 30 per cent and 20 per cent for the two provinces containing its largest cities to less than one per cent in a very rural province. Young girls are often kept at home to look after their younger siblings, especially in rural areas. By taking on this task, ECD programmes 'free' the girls to attend school.

2.2.2. Non-formal Basic Education Activities

Non-formal basic education activities in rural areas target various groups of illiterate and semi-literate adults, as well as children and adolescents unenrolled in school. Most non-formal education activities in rural areas probably include a component to develop literacy and numeracy skills. This may be the primary focus, or an instrumental element contributing to other objectives, such as improved health, income generation or food security. The variety of non-formal programmes is as vast as the range of their sponsors. Most are small-scale activities organised by community associations or other non-governmental organisations and some are organised by provincial or local authorities.

Relatively few non-formal education programmes are organised by central governments, probably reflecting the priority they give to running the formal education system, which already draws heavily on their resources and management capacity. There are a few encouraging examples of non-formal programmes that have expanded to reach large numbers of rural communities. One of the best known examples is the non-governmental Bangladesh Rural Advancement Committee (BRAC), which began providing rural non-formal schooling in 1985. By 1998 it operated some thirty-four thousand schools serving more than 1.2 million children.

Some other programmes, like the rural radio stations in southern Mali, make use of radio or other media in the vernacular current in rural areas to inform various rural target groups and promote their basic learning in respect to health, agricultural practices, child care, environmental issues, etc. It is clear, however, that non-formal programmes of all sizes have made and continue to make a significant contribution to meeting basic learning needs of rural people. The 'non-formality' or flexibility of such programmes enables them to reach groups or to meet learning needs that are overlooked by government departments and services. Public authorities and external donors often acknowledge the impact of such programmes in specific communities and districts. While there is certainly room and a need for expansion of good, non-formal basic education programmes, they are unlikely to reach the scale required to meet the vast unmet basic learning needs of large numbers of rural children and adults.

Although insufficient funding is the principal limitation on the expansion of non-formal programmes, their very nature makes it difficult to scale them up without 'formalising' them and compromising certain of their advantages, such as flexibility, adaptability and constructive interaction with the learners and the local community. However, public authorities could certainly encourage and support such initiatives to a far greater extent and examine their experiences for innovations that might be applied in schooling and extension programmes run by public institutions.

2.2.3. Improving the Provision of Basic Education

2.2.3.1. Basic Education with Greater Equity

A large proportion of the world's rural population has little or no access to basic education offered by the state or by other education providers. According to UNESCO, there are well over 100 million primary school-age children unenrolled in the schools of the less developed countries, and most of them are from poor families in rural areas. Unfortunately, many of the children who do enrol in school drop out without obtaining a viable basic education, and even those children who do complete the primary cycle need further learning opportunities, which are even more scarce than schooling in rural areas. Only a small fraction of rural adolescents and adults have access to any organised basic education programme.

2.2.3.2. Constructing more Primary Schools and Classrooms

Constructing more primary schools and classrooms in rural areas is an obvious priority for many countries. A parallel strategy to increase school capacity is to seek ways to use existing facilities and teachers more efficiently to accommodate more pupils. Where feasible, for instance, multigrade classrooms and teaching pupils in shifts (e.g. one set of pupils in the morning, another set in the afternoon) can effectively expand the school system's capacity.

While the physical expansion of the primary school system will certainly enable more children to have access to schooling, meeting the basic learning needs of the marginalised and neglected groups and categories of learners will require additional, special efforts. Among the children unenrolled in school, girls still constitute the majority, despite the priority given to girls' education in numerous international and national policy instruments.

Other groups and categories whose basic learning needs generally are not met include very young (pre-school) children, working children (more visible in urban areas but present in rural areas, too), illiterate adults, remote and nomadic populations, refugees and people with disabilities who have special learning needs. Providing suitable learning opportunities for these children, adolescents and adults in rural areas is certainly a challenge, especially for the low income countries, but it must be met in order truly to achieve Education for All. Various initiatives over the past few decades have shown promising ways to reach certain of these target groups with basic education services.

2.2.3.3. *Making Primary Education Compulsory*

Making primary education compulsory is an important prerequisite for achieving EFA. Legislation governing education in some countries needs to be reviewed and revised to make compulsory education attainable and enforceable in rural areas. Any remaining legal impediments to girls' education, for instance, must be removed.

Certain administrative requirements and practices, such as possession of an official birth certificate in order to enrol in school, also constitute obstacles for many rural families. Appropriate legal and administrative measures can eliminate such obstacles. Likewise, laws and customs concerning the legal age for first marriage and governing child labour may also need to be revised to remove another set of obstacles to girls' and boys' participation in schooling.

2.2.3.4. *Increasing the School Enrolment of Girls*

Increasing the school enrolment of girls is a priority aim for many governments. Of course any increase in the number of schools and classrooms should enable more girls, as well as boys, to enrol in school. However, experience has shown that increasing the proportion of girls enrolled, as well as their numbers—thereby moving toward better male/ female equity in schooling—often requires special measures to induce parents to enrol their daughters and keep them in school.

Some relatively simple changes can often make a big difference. For example, enclosing the schoolyard with a fence and building a separate latrine for girls can help allay parental concerns for their daughters' safety. Another simple measure is adjusting the school calendar to accommodate other demands on girls' time, such as fetching water early in the morning or selling goods on the weekly market day.

Teaching is still a male-dominated profession in many low-income countries and in some societies, rural families are reluctant to entrust their daughters to a male teacher. Several countries have succeeded in boosting the enrolment and retention of rural girls in school by recruiting more women teachers for rural assignments. This measure is not without complications, however, as young, unmarried women are often reluctant to go to rural areas, especially if they are not of the same ethnic or language group. Recruiting young women to serve as teachers in their own village or area is sometimes a viable solution and offers positive role models with which the local girls can more easily identify.

In addition to appropriate changes in the curriculum, any gender-biased behaviour of teachers, especially but not only male teachers, should be corrected through training and supervision. Girl pupils ignored or ridiculed during math lessons, for example, are candidates for drop-out. Overcoming cultural resistance to girls' education and compensating families for the opportunity costs they incur when girls attend school generally require even more demanding solutions.

Information campaigns to sensitise parents to the benefits of girls' education may achieve some positive results, but are more effective if they are accompanied by some incentive scheme such as offering cash 'scholarships' to families who enrol their daughters in school. Scholarships and other financial incentives such as the waiving of school fees and providing free textbooks for girls can encourage poor families to allow at least one daughter to attend school -an important first step in opening a rural school to girls. When such incentive schemes are planned and conducted in consultation with local families, the positive effects on girls' participation in schooling are more likely to carry on even when the financial incentives finally end.

2.2.3.5. *School-feeding Programmes*

School-feeding programmes, which provide a midday meal and/ or mid-morning snack for pupils, boys and girls, can be an effective incentive for enrolment and attendance in school. In the initial negotiations with the local community, an increase in girls' participation in schooling can be made a condition for the introduction of such a programme.

The provision of nutritious food to children at school may produce health benefits as well, particularly in rural areas with low food security. There is some evidence that it also helps improve children's concentration in class and thereby presumably improves their learning achievement. The World Food Programme (WFP), which has supported schoolfeeding programmes in numerous countries for several decades, finds takehome food rations effectively promote girls' education.

Due to dramatic increases in enrolment at the onset of many food aid programmes, student enrolment levels should be monitored as the educational quality and supporting infrastructures may take longer to establish. Recent studies, however, show that school-feeding programmes actually increase government involvement and may help create increased attention and funding to these key issues.

These early childhood years are when experiences and interactions with parents, family members and other adults influence the way a child's brain develops, with as much impact as such factors as adequate nutrition, good health and clean water. And how the child develops during this period sets the stage for later success in school and the character of adolescence and adulthood.

Poor families with little or no education are ill equipped to provide the kinds of stimulation young children need to develop their latent capacities. ECD programmes can help parents become better 'educators' and can directly provide educational activities and child-care services while the parents work. ECD pre-school programmes for children in the 4 to 6 age group are generally credited with preparing children for structured, group learning in school.

Providing care and education for young orphans is becoming a major task for African governments. Armed conflicts in poor countries have generated millions of orphans, as well as injured, disabled and homeless children. Natural disasters and devastating diseases have added to this pool of especially vulnerable children.

2.2.3.6. Basic Education for Working Children

In rural areas, children can be seen tending flocks, working in the fields, running errands in the villages, doing household chores, minding young children and working at various crafts. Some forms of child labour are clearly hazardous and harmful, such as the young banana pickers in Ecuador, some as young as eight, who are exposed to the spraying of toxic chemicals and to sexual harassment, according to a recent report by Human Rights Watch. However, other tasks performed by children in rural areas are not detrimental in themselves, are useful to their families and may entail some basic learning that is well suited to local conditions and employment opportunities.

Yet, children who remain illiterate, with little or no exposure to the range of subjects offered in the school, are poorly equipped to improve their livelihood and living conditions and to adapt to changes in the rural economy. Most countries have legislation for a defined period of compulsory education (e.g. the first 5 or 6 grades of primary schooling, or from age 6 through 12), but enforcement, particularly in rural areas, is problematic. Poor families often depend on their children's labour and whatever additional income they can earn.

Forcing their children to attend school -even if this could be done—would undermine the viability of many poor families. The more humane approach is to find ways to adapt the school to their needs or to provide alternative opportunities to acquire basic education. Some adjustment of school hours and the school calendar may also enable some working children to attend at least part-time.

Similarly, school feeding and other incentive schemes can help compensate families for the labour or income foregone when their children attend school instead of working. A careful needs analysis undertaken in consultation with local families and local authorities can help identify which adjustments, if any, could attract and retain working children in school.

Such locally negotiated adjustments to schooling may not always be feasible or fully effective. Offering working children an alternative to conventional schooling requires more planning and effort, but can achieve good results.

2.2.3.7. Basic Education for Illiterate Adults

Illiterate adults and others who have weak literacy and numeracy skills constitute a very large target group for adult basic education (ABE). This is clearly an important dimension of Education for All and can also be a strategic factor in the transformation of rural areas. There is some evidence of a revival of interest in ABE among donors.

Earlier disappointment with the results of literacy campaigns and programmes seems to be giving way to a growing recognition of the several important benefits and outcomes of well designed ABE programmes. A recent report published by the World Bank notes that: "Earlier allegations about generally poor internal efficiency of ABE are contradicted by the bulk of evidence now available." It goes on to say that minimum literacy can be achieved at less cost among motivated youth and adults than the cost of three or four years of primary schooling.

Various studies and programme evaluations have established significant outcomes attributed to ABE beyond the acquisition of literacy and numeracy skills. It is not surprising, for example, that literate mothers generally see to it that their sons and daughters become literate, too. There are definite correlations between parental education levels and children's school enrolment, attendance and learning achievement.

Literacy and numeracy are directly useful in the marketplace and in management tasks, so these skills, together with certain other ABE content, can lead to more productive livelihoods—an essential factor in alleviating poverty. Considerable research and experimentation has gone into developing effective pedagogies for use with adults. Those that appear more successful seek to be participatory, respecting the adult learner, who brings considerable life experience and (usually) strong motivation to the learning situation. This pedagogical approach helps build the learner's selfconfidence and develops positive group dynamics. However, it demands very competent teachers, so it is difficult to apply on a large scale.

Many ABE programmes even avoid using the term 'teacher', with its connotation of schooling, preferring terms like 'facilitator' or 'co-ordinator' that imply the learning group is composed of peers, each making a contribution. This is an important feature of the REFLECT approach to literacy learning, which was developed during the 1990s and is now being used in many low-income countries, particularly in rural areas and helps to ensure that literacy programmes are relevant to the needs of the rural people and are planned and managed in a participatory way.

Many ABE programmes use a functional literacy approach, which seeks to develop literacy and numeracy skills in a context that is meaningful and motivational to the learners. Some focus on specific issues or skills, such as health, food security or bee keeping, with literacy and numeracy as subordinate objectives. One such programme in Nicaragua used videos as the main training tool, supplemented by simple print materials, to show rural farmers how to raise iguanas, a high protein traditional dish.

In the low-income countries, the main providers of basic education for adults are voluntary organisations and local community associations, often with support from international NGOs and funding agencies. Some governments have set up special departments or mechanisms to promote literacy activities, such as Tamil Nadu's Total Literacy Campaign.

Funding is often directed to some mix of programmes run by NGOs and perhaps others run directly by public authorities (e.g. agricultural extension service, ministry of health). In other cases, government and NGOs divide responsibilities for ABE according to their respective comparative advantage, usually with NGOs and local community associations in direct contact with the adult learners. Senegal, for instance, has an established framework for government-NGO co-operation in ABE. Such arrangements can encourage and facilitate NGO initiatives, while enabling the public authorities to orient ABE activities towards general policy objectives.

In defining a priority or target group for an ABE programme, many providers use age as one criterion, giving preference, for example, to adolescents and adults in the productive and reproductive age range of approximately 15 to 45. Women, especially young mothers, are targeted often because of their role in the household (e.g. cooking, childcare, kitchen gardening) and the multiplier effect on other family members. Some ABE programmes target specific vocational or functional categories (e.g. farmers, craftsmen, village leaders) that correspond to their content.

With few exceptions, the mass literacy campaigns of earlier years have been abandoned in favour of longer-term and more structured ABE programmes. However, campaigns to raise public awareness of the importance of literacy can be useful in preparing and supporting ABE programmes. ABE is an investment that deserves far more attention, effort and resources than it currently receives.

2.2.3.8. Basic Education in Remote Areas

Remote rural populations are neglected or under-served by the school system in many low-income countries. In addition to the geographical factors that tend to isolate them, people living in remote rural areas may be further marginalised from the mainstream by ethnicity, culture, language, or religion, as well as their material poverty. The centrally determined school curriculum may appear to them as quite irrelevant to their very different basic learning needs.

A recent case study of remote highland communities in Thailand noted a growing awareness of the need to harmonise modern knowledge and local wisdom. Consequently, to maintain the socio-cultural heritage and integrity through inter-generation communication, the importance of local curriculum development is recognised by a number of communities, as well as concerned governmental and non-governmental organisations.

Where cultural differences are not a factor and where roads, communications and other infrastructure reach into remote areas, providing schools and other basic education facilities is largely a matter of political will and allocation of sufficient resources. The situation in many other low-income countries is quite different from that of Cuba, however, with important cultural differences and a lack of physical and administrative infrastructures impeding or limiting the provision of basic education in remote areas.

Nomadic Peoples

Nomadic peoples, unlike most marginalised groups in remote rural areas, have a distinct lifestyle that sets them apart from the sedentary 'host population'. They are often desperately poor in material terms, and subject to the vagaries of the climate. In addition, they may differ from the majority population by ethnicity, religion and language. Such differences can be a source of antagonism, mistrust and even conflict between them. The sedentary population may consider nomads as 'foreigners' with an inferior, primitive way of life. These attitudes can influence public policy towards them, which in turn delimits the ways and means employed to meet their basic learning needs.

In Africa, the general policy of governments in respect to nomadic peoples is not spelled out clearly but appears in practice to seek to settle them and adapt them to the modern economy. Some governments place restrictions on the nomadic way of life or simply neglect them, perhaps in the expectation that sooner or later they will have to settle down and become normal citizens.

Whatever the educational goals may be, the generally low participation rate of nomads reflects their differing perspective as to the value of education programmes. According to one analysis, education providers attribute low enrolment to parental ignorance, the low motivation of teachers and the logistical problems caused by nomadic mobility and remoteness, whereas nomads are bothered by the alien language and culture imposed on their children. Similarly, providers attribute high dropout rates to parental conservatism, child labour and curriculum irrelevance, while nomads withdraw their children because they perceive schooling to be of low quality, exclude parental involvement and provide a risk-prone and hostile environment.

Most observers would probably agree that schooling, especially through boarding schools, tends to undermine nomadic culture and traditional values, but its threat to the economic structure of pastoralism, which depends on household and collective responsibilities (versus the individualism of Western education), is less evident.

Apart from the issues of policy and perceptions regarding education, providing basic education to nomadic groups involves some major challenges in respect to content and logistics. There is abundant evidence that nomads value literacy and numeracy skills, but other elements of the nationally prescribed curriculum may appear less useful to them. The lack of curriculum relevance is often cited as a major reason for the low participation and completion rates of nomadic children.

This suggests that nomads need to be much more involved in planning the curriculum designed for their children. A related matter is the medium of instruction. Using the prevalent mother tongue can help strengthen the group's cultural identity, whereas use of a national language may help integrate the group more closely with the mainstream national culture—or alienate the nomads further. This seems another matter well worth negotiating with the group concerned.

Providing schools with boarding facilities, though a costly option, has been used with mixed success in some countries. Parents are often reluctant to lose the custody and household labour of their sons and daughters and to entrust them to people they don't know. The success of boarding schools depends on the quality of life within the school and the effective security (physical and moral) in and around it. However, in rural areas of low food security, fixed location schools with a feeding programme become attractive.

A mobile school seems, in principle, a more promising solution, but it has also proved problematic. Administrative difficulties, combined with shortcomings in the design and maintenance of collapsible classrooms and the reluctance of some teachers to adapt to a nomadic lifestyle have undermined the planned use of mobile schools in some cases, as in Nigeria.

Theoretically, some secular subjects could be added to the 'curriculum' of Koranic schools where public schools are not available, but this entails convincing and training the Koranic teachers, and supplying them with appropriate instructional materials. Such an arrangement is being used in some settled rural communities in the state of Uttar Pradesh in India, whereby a literacy component is now included in the Muslim schools.

Open and distance learning (ODL) seems to offer another promising approach to reach nomadic peoples, but so far it has had limited impact, at least in Africa. ODL can offer nomads (adults as well as children) on the move access to education, which can be designed with the flexibility needed to fit their lifestyle. Several technologies and delivery models have been used, including radio broadcasts, mobile cinema, audio cassettes and printed materials, combined with self-help study groups, mobile schools and fixed location schools.

In many cases, non-formal delivery of basic education to nomadic peoples may be more suitable than formal schooling. Successful non-formal programmes were found to have all or some of the following features:

- delivery within a non-antagonistic, cultural and human environment;
- two-way processes, flexible in structure and content, to respond to changing needs;
- providing skills designed to increase nomads' control over social, economic and political obstacles to their livelihood security (e.g. lobbying, local advocacy);
- linkages with existing government institutions for education and development;
- and informal settings of the learning environment that allow parents' close surveillance over children's security, especially of girls.

Refugees and Internally Displaced Persons (IDPs)

Refugees and internally displaced persons (IDPs) uprooted from their homes by natural disasters or by civil conflicts constitute yet another heterogeneous category of people found in rural areas and who have little or no access to established education services. The world refugee population was estimated to be some 11.5 million in 1998 and the number of IDPs may be around 50 million. Thirty-nine countries have displaced populations exceeding 50,000. Although some refugees flee from urban areas, most refugee camps are located in rural areas, sometimes in quite remote areas, usually near a frontier.

Most refugee camps do have schools, but they often lack learning materials and trained teachers. Many camps also have some ECD programme and some literacy and vocational training classes for adolescents and adults.

Few low-income countries are adequately prepared or have contingency plans to deal with an influx of refugees or with an internal emergency situation. Fortunately, there are several international agencies and non-governmental organisations that have valuable experience and access to resources to assist governments in emergency situations. Each emergency or crisis is unique in some respects, so the appropriate educational response needs to be worked out on a case-by-case basis, preferably in consultation with the population groups concerned. In general, though, these education interventions need to be planned from the beginning as part of a development process that contributes to post-emergency reconstruction of the disrupted education system and to social reconciliation.

Children and Adults with Disabilities

Children and adults with disabilities constitute a transversal category whose learning needs are not met well or at all, especially in rural areas. To some extent, these learners face a double discrimination. They are excluded from basic education programmes because of physical, mental or behavioural impairments—or because of negative attitudes in respect to their impairments and they are penalised by the rest of the rural people.

Some face exclusion also because of gender, ethnicity, geographical isolation and/or poverty. The World Education Forum advocated a more thoughtful approach to inclusive education, which has been defined as a set of processes to increase participation in education and reduce exclusion. Although inclusive education is commonly assumed to imply that learners should be physically in the same place and doing the same activities, another interpretation views inclusion as social acceptance and belonging, with a right to individually relevant learning.

However, many disabled learners can be accommodated in existing schools and non-formal programmes with a reasonable amount of flexibility and goodwill. Sensitising, encouraging and training school and programme administrators and teachers to recognise and deal with disabilities is a prerequisite to providing basic education opportunities to people with disabilities.

Special learning materials are needed in some cases, e.g. reading material in Braille for blind learners and a few donor agencies are experienced in providing technical and financial assistance for this purpose. Early detection of actual or latent disabilities can often lead to treatment that reduces their gravity and enables the child or adult to participate in learning activities with little or no special attention. Simple screening for visual or hearing impairments, for example, may save a child's schooling.

In some rural communities, a programme to sensitise and inform parents about possible disabilities, their treatment and their effects, if any, on a child's ability to learn can help draw out children with disabilities who otherwise may be kept at home because of a sense of shame or ignorance.

2.2.3.9. Relevance of the Curricula

The relevance of the curricula used in primary schooling and other basic education programmes in rural areas determines their appeal to learners and their effectiveness at meeting basic learning needs. Defining what is 'basic' and what are true 'needs' is not always evident. Most learners, whether children or adults, want and expect to learn to read and write and manipulate numbers, but their expectations regarding other content and skills can vary. There are four guidelines for designing basic education content for learners in rural areas.

First, the curriculum should relate to the local context, customs, livelihoods and rural development activities. Second, it should take due account of the teachers' qualifications and training (although ideally these should be in accord with the curriculum). Third, it should make use of locally available skills, knowledge and other resources. Fourth, it should respond to the expressed wishes of the community (i.e. be demand-driven), determined through consultation and negotiation with the community, or the adult learners.

The inclusion of skills relating to livelihoods will certainly attract adolescent and adult learners, but they may request and appreciate less utilitarian content as well, such as history, music and religion. Some educators advocate including subjects such as human rights, avoidance and resolution of conflicts, HIV/AIDS and other health topics. Whatever the configuration of content may be, basic education should equip learners to continue learning, apply critical thinking and cope with the changes they will encounter in life.

However, the primary school curriculum is usually determined at the national level and designed for urban pupils.

Often it is packed with subjects, each useful in itself but constituting together a heavy load for even the cleverest pupil. Non-formal programmes often achieve better learning results by focusing on a few core subjects. The margin for adaptation of the curriculum to fit local learning needs is often limited, but school heads and other supervisors can be encouraged to seek and allow more flexibility in applying the curriculum in rural areas.

The Escuela Nueva (New School) programme developed in Latin America over the past 30 years demonstrates that it is definitely possible to achieve a functional balance in the basic education curriculum that respects national criteria and responds to local rural conditions. This and similar initiatives combine the national common core content and supplementary content based on the local culture and economy, often making use of local artisans, story-tellers, and other human resources in the community.

2.2.3.10. Language of Instruction

Language of instruction represents an important factor affecting the perceived relevance of a basic education programme, as well as its effectiveness. Instruction in the mother tongue certainly facilitates learning in the early stages. However, it may be necessary—and expected—that another language (the official language or another of wide usage) be introduced into the curriculum at a later stage, particularly if there is little or no literature in the mother tongue. Parents have been known to object to their children being 'excluded' from learning in a dominant language. Whatever the case, the teacher should be fully fluent in the language of instruction and learning materials in that language should be available in the classroom.

2.2.3.11. Learning Materials

Learning materials constitute an important input to basic education that is generally deficient, both in quality and quantity, in rural areas. Classrooms without useable blackboards, maps, or charts are common. Textbooks, readers, writing slates, exercise books, chalk, pencils and pens are too often in short supply. Even the teacher may have no course guides or resource materials. Efforts to improve the quality and outcomes of basic education need to give early attention to these material supports for learning.

2.2.3.12. *Educational Facilities*

Educational facilities, i.e. the buildings and grounds, are an important factor in shaping the learning environment. A well maintained building, suited to the climate, with attractive, well furnished classrooms and good ventilation and lighting, facilitates the teaching-learning process. Safe drinking water, separate toilets for girls and boys and electricity should become normal features of rural schools and other learning centres. The playground and school garden also serve for learning activities. All of these features of a good learning environment (with the possible exception of the supply of electricity) should be manageable in most rural communities. Careful consultation with local leaders and parents, possibly together with some form of incentive (e.g. food for work), can lead to the school being 'owned' and managed by the local community.

2.2.3.13. *Information and Communication Technologies (ICTs)*

Information and communication technologies (ICTs), especially radio, are being used in several countries to support schooling and adult basic education programmes in rural areas. However, their potential is still largely untapped. The efficacy of radio as a support for in-service teacher training is generally acknowledged, but its use in the classroom or adult learning centre can be problematic (e.g. scheduling of broadcasts, interference with reception, supplying batteries for transistor radios).

Televised broadcasts are used more rarely to reach rural learners. Audio and video cassettes are more readily utilised and have certain advantages, such as local scheduling, possible interruption and immediate playback for understanding, etc. The use of these technologies in basic education needs to be moderated by a teacher for best results. In spite of their merits and potential, the contribution of ITCs on achieving EFA goals still remains to be assessed. Cost-effectiveness is one of the issues that need to be better captured.

2.2.3.14. *Assessing Learning Achievement*

Assessing learning achievement at given intervals can help both the teacher and the learner to measure progress in the learning process. When properly done in a non-threatening manner, tests can be an effective pedagogical tool, encouraging learners to make their best effort. Test results also help supervisors and administrators to detect weaknesses in the curriculum or in teaching or in other inputs and to take corrective measures as needed.

Both standardised testing and continuous assessment of learning are especially problematic in rural areas due to logistical difficulties and the usually deficient training of rural teachers. The next section, which deals with general management issues, will discuss ways to deal with this problem.

2.2.4. Planning Basic Education for Rural Development

2.2.4.1. Monitoring Basic Education Activities

Monitoring basic education activities in rural areas is a prerequisite for planning and implementing reforms or improvements. Basic statistics on the school-age population, enrolments, attendance, completion and promotion are essential for good management of the school system, but are often incomplete and flawed for rural areas. These and other quantitative and qualitative data, broken down by gender, community, type of schooling, administrative area and other appropriate categories, are useful in detecting disparities and malfunctions that require corrective action.

Analysis of these data can reveal urban/rural disparities, but also the differences and diversity among rural areas that are needed for planning and management decisions at sub-national level. The results of such analyses, if properly utilised, can inform policy decisions that affect the allocation and use of resources for basic education in rural areas.

The standardised testing of learning achievement can provide important information on the performance of schools. Senior managers of the school system may use test results as one criterion in determining the allocation of human and material resources. With equity in educational opportunity now a key policy objective, disparities in test results that favour urban areas should incite compensatory investments in rural schooling.

Monitoring non-formal education activities in rural areas is particularly problematic, especially those activities operated by NGOs and local community associations. Where government provides funding or other support, providers can be required to file periodic reports including data items, such as numbers of beneficiaries by age and gender, that are useful for planning and management purposes. Another option is conducting sample surveys to obtain illustrative data on the nature, scope, organisation and outcomes of non-formal basic education activities in selected rural areas.

2.2.4.2. *Eliminating Urban/rural Disparities*

Eliminating urban/rural disparities in basic education requires comprehensive planning within the overall education and training system, so that basic education in rural areas can offer relevant learning opportunities equivalent in quality to those accessible in urban areas. Its formal and non-formal components should be designed and managed to be complementary and, insofar as possible, they should be integrated with other rural development initiatives (e.g. to improve health, food security, agricultural production, protection of the environment, local autonomy, access to credit, etc.).

Mechanisms for periodic consultation and joint planning among key actors should help achieve this harmonisation. School mapping, for example, should take into account the analyses and plans of various rural development specialists, who in turn could be called upon to help with the in-service training of education personnel employed in formal and nonformal programmes in rural areas. Conversely, rural extension workers could be sensitised to identify unmet basic learning needs and to dialogue with teachers and administrators of education and training activities.

Further synergies can be fostered at community level by using the school as a centre for social activities relating to rural development. The development of basic education in rural areas needs to be planned and carried out in a long-term and systemic perspective. Shifts in policy and approaches should be minimal in order to establish and retain essential coherence in the provision of basic education services. A study in Senegal, for example, concluded that "a lack of coherence in the strategies" had been a major shortcoming in the development of basic education in rural areas since independence.

Innovations are usually introduced tentatively in a limited area, with exceptionally high levels of resources (often donor supplied and driven). This experimentation with innovations is prudent and useful, but few 'successes' are then widely replicated or expanded to scale, incorporated into the national education and training system or even continued beyond the experimental period. Obviously, more thought and commitment should be given to going to scale with successful innovations and putting them on a firm and sustainable basis.

Eliminating disparities does not imply homogenisation of the teachinglearning process nor of its specific content. As seen in earlier sections, there is great diversity in rural areas, both in local situations (economy, language, customs, values) and in the basic learning needs of various groups of learners. Some mix of common subject matter set at the national level with locally determined elements can improve a programme's relevance and attractiveness to rural learners. Likewise, teaching aids and methods adapted to the local community and making use of available resources can enhance the learning process. Local conditions may require also flexibility in the school (or programme) calendar, class hours and the language of instruction. Many non-formal education programmes already demonstrate such adaptability to conditions in rural areas.

Involving local communities in the planning and implementation processes can more easily achieve such diversity in the provision of basic education. On this point, one analysis recommends "...a bottom-up planning process through which rural communities express themselves and their views are consolidated and co-ordinated at the local/district government level. These then need to be compiled and collated across districts, regions, states/provinces and finally at the national level. Such an approach would reflect on-ground realities and allow a network to be built in which local, regional and national perspectives would be reconciled".

2.2.4.3. *Targeting Funding*

Targeting funding where it is most needed is clearly essential, but often difficult to do because of bureaucratic constraints and vested interests. Pushing such choices to lower levels by decentralising responsibility for basic education may make funding decisions more sensitive to local needs, but it may also open the door for abuses that would be more difficult to conceal at higher administrative levels. Another controversial measure deserves mention here. Appropriate funding schemes might be devised both to raise additional local resources and to give priority to schools or communities most in need, for example by using coefficients related to low school enrolment or survival rates, adult illiteracy rates, or other indicators of need.

Formula funding has been used in many school systems to determine resource allocations. The physical location of the school is sometimes taken into consideration to provide extra resources—staff or budget—to isolated schools. Within the state budget for primary schooling, some rethinking of allocations could help rectify current urban/rural disparities. For example, incentives in the form of salary differentials, subsidised housing, food and transportation allowances and opportunities for professional advancement could be introduced to make rural teaching assignments more attractive.

Funding for the training and support of rural school principals can be an investment in making schools more effective. Providing modest discretionary funds for rural schools to use to improve the learning environment, as tried out in India, can help raise standards and morale. More investment in providing teaching aids and learning materials to rural schools would certainly produce good returns in learning achievement and completion rates.

In communities where formal schooling is not yet feasible or where there is a pool of out-of-school children and illiterate adolescents and adults, non-formal basic education programmes are the obvious alternative. As seen earlier, radio and audio- and videocassettes have proved effective educational media in several rural situations (e.g. nomads, isolated groups) and thus offer an investment possibility that can sometimes be a cost-effective means to reach certain disadvantaged groups. When considering the targeting or allocation of funding, one must beware of thinking in either/or terms. All target groups need attention. All forms of basic education need resources. The issue is really to find a viable and effective dosage that works for equity and contributes to rural development.

2.2.4.4. Promoting Community Ownership

Promoting community ownership of basic education programmes helps ensure their relevance, sustainability and effectiveness both in terms of learning achievement and of contributing to other rural development objectives. Involving local communities in the planning process is a first step and this needs to be done in an open, inclusive way so that all interest groups can express their views and any potential opposition is removed or at least identified.

In view of the various obstacles to basic education discussed earlier, achieving community ownership can often be a very delicate matter, which may require determined and patient negotiation skills by education providers. A further complication is due to the fact that conflicts of interest among groups exist in most communities. In some instances government has a role to play in balancing individuals' rights and community responsibility.

Consequently, any decentralisation of responsibility for basic education needs to be worked out carefully to guard against possible domination and discrimination at local levels. The Community Learning Centres operating in the Asia and Pacific region exemplify a particularly flexible approach to providing non-formal education opportunities that depend largely on local initiative and resources.

A reasonable balance must be found between government support and supervision on one hand and community ownership on the other. Ownership often entailed allocation of resources by the community, but these resources should be additional and not seen as a substitute for government funding and other support. In fact, communities in neglected rural areas of many low-income countries have taken the initiative to create their own schools. While admirable in itself, this kind of local ownership can pose a dilemma in terms of equity and in relation to the right to education:

> "...national school systems should distribute resources equitably to all schools, rural and urban. As long as poor rural communities finance their own schools, government resources to education are inequitably allocated to urban schools, where, ironically, families can probably afford to pay more. If the ministry builds and furnishes a school in the [rural] community, parents may stop paying as much, but they may also lose control".

Community ownership can be enhanced also by involving local secular and religious leaders, if not as direct participants (e.g. in adult literacy classes), then as sponsors or members of the local education council. Similarly, linking basic education programmes, especially those for adults, to local social institutions and groups (e.g. temples, mosques, churches, women's associations) can draw support from existing loyalties and help ensure the programmes' sustainability. Programme or school oversight committees and parent-teacher associations are other ways of involving community members in the management of basic education programmes.

In Uganda, for instance, 'core' schools are linked to 'outreach' schools. China offers another example with its 'twinning' arrangements that link schools in the developed coastal areas with schools in the poorer areas in the west of the country.

2.2.4.5. *Role of Non-governmental Organisations and Community Associations*

Non-governmental organisations and community associations constitute another set of important actors in providing basic education opportunities in rural areas. They are often the only providers of nonformal basic education in rural communities and many operate with little or no government support. Some NGOs have generated innovative approaches that have been replicated widely, e.g. REFLECT, while others have had significant influence on public policy regarding literacy and other non-formal basic education programmes. The initiative, flexibility, dedication and resources NGOs bring to rural areas often make a significant contribution to basic education and to rural development.

In many remote rural areas, NGOs are the only providers of public services, including education. The training of NGO personnel, the monitoring and evaluation of NGO programmes, and the planning for replicability and scaling up, or, in other words, the sustainability of NGO programmes need special attention and support. The actual and potential contribution of NGOs make them valuable actors in rural areas that can be brought into a sound working partnership with government and other actors. This is essential for any major expansion of non-formal basic education programmes for adolescents and adults.

In the low-income countries, private sector involvement in education is most evident, if at all, in the number of private schools, which varies widely among countries. Many private schools are managed by religious organisations and may have a particular religious agenda as well as offering the state determined curriculum. Other private schools are run on a forprofit basis and have higher costs (and often higher standards) than the public schools.

The private sector is generally much less involved in nonformal basic education. Some small rural enterprises do provide facilities or material support for literacy and non-formal vocational training programmes. A few enlightened employers realise that literacy and numeracy skills can improve the performance, health and safety of their workers, and are willing to support or even organise literacy programmes for them.

References

Govinda, R; Varghese, N.V., *Quality of primary schooling in India: a case study of Madhya Pradesh,* Paris: IIEP-UNESCO, 1993.

Janke, C., *Food and Education. background considerations for policy and programming,* Catholic Relief Services, 2001.

Moulton, J., *Improving education in rural areas: guidance for rural development specialists* (draft), Washington DC: World Bank, 2001.

Reddy, B.S., *Education and rural development in rural India,* Paris: IIEP-UNESCO, 2001.

World Food Programme, *School feeding works for girls' education,* Rome: WFP, 2001.

World Bank, *Effective schooling in rural communities. Key topics,* Washington DC: World Bank, 2000.

3

Innovative Approaches in Rural Education

3.1. Students Environment

Students' environment and experience, including agriculture, can be used as a means of enhancing the learning process and learning outcomes through a what is sometimes called a 'contextualised' approach. Agriculture has been included as a component of primary school education in many countries, but it has acquired a poor reputation with many stakeholders in education. One major reason for this is the association of agriculture subjects and experience with unproductive labour and little educational value.

Learning is much influenced by the relationship between three distinct environments; the home, the school and the community. This approach suggests that the content of education programmes, the methods by which learning is facilitated and the materials used to this end should be pertinent to the experience, culture and environment of the learners. In other words, teaching and learning should be contextualised.

3.1.1. Contextualisation of Learning

The contextualised approaches are used and do work in many education initiatives in different countries, although it is still extremely rare to find interventions where contextualisation of teaching and learning is the main focus. Some examples are also given from a very wide range of projects in rural schools. These are selected on the basis that they contain elements of support to teaching and learning that could be described as contextualisation. It is clear that contextualisation of learning in rural schools is a strategy which has been attempted in various educational programmes, illustrated by those examples above where an effort has been made to relate the content of the curriculum to the local environment. A number of difficulties are shown to be associated with this, including the constraints placed upon teachers by workload, general conditions and lack of experience as well as the driving force of examination-oriented learning which acts against the introduction of more flexible approaches to teaching and learning.

However, the potential benefits of contextualising learning in rural schools are great, provided constraints are minimised and efforts are taken to build on what already exists, namely the reality of the local context. Since agriculture forms the reality for many rural dwellers around the world.

3.1.1.1. Role of Agriculture

It is clear that agriculture can play a powerful role in the wider learning process in rural schools. An agricultural topic used as a medium for contextualising part of the curriculum can provide an avenue through which children can have repeated experiences which help them to master cognitive, physical and social skills. Agriculture can be the basis of integrated projects incorporated in the school curriculum, with academic activities chosen for their locally relevant, experimental attributes.

For example, the Department of Primary Education, Sri Lanka, advocates strongly the use of agricultural experience as a medium for contextualisation and have maintained their emphasis on its importance in the recent national programme of curriculum development:

The success of the teaching-learning process depends heavily on the motivation of both the learner and the teacher. It has been identified that information regarding food habits and types of food of the community can be used in introducing innovative strategies in education. Outdoor activities using agricultural plots in the school and the home can also make learning more meaningful and hence attractive.

Even though the agricultural experience of individuals will differ, agriculture can still be used as a vehicle to make school learning more meaningful. Metaphors and analogies can be based on agricultural activities and experiences and thus enhance the acquisition of literacy, numeracy and the skills of basic scientific reasoning within the confines of a subjectbased curriculum. Children may be encouraged to relate the learning process in school with the natural learning process which exists outside the classroom and begin to provide the means by which the process of learning becomes continuous, in school and beyond.

At home, many pupils will be involved in daily agricultural practices such as feeding and herding livestock, watering, digging and weeding. Agricultural seasons may also affect the pupils' school attendance record. This familiarity with agriculture may provide a basis for contextualizing learning over a range of subjects. It can enable children to develop not only basic knowledge and skills, but also higher-order competencies, such as problem-solving and thinking skills and broader competencies such as leadership skills, group skills and personal initiative.

In several schools, pupils brought in agricultural materials such as plants, seeds or foodstuffs, which were then used by teachers to help explain abstract mathematical concepts. In interviews, both teachers and pupils indicated ways in which use of agricultural experience had assisted them in understanding some aspect of the curriculum. A teacher in Tanzania cited an example of teaching English to his pupils where he was attempting to explain the word 'bunch'. Pupils had difficulty grasping the meaning of this term until they were taken outside and shown a bunch of bananas on a tree. According to the teacher, "my teaching aids are outside ... it makes a picture and the pupils understand".

An Indian mathematics teacher described how he had taken pupils into the rice field opposite the school to illustrate to pupils how straight lines and angles were used in practice. Another teacher said that he could refer to sheep in lessons on counting, as many of the pupils herded sheep. Where pupils were required to learn about wild animals, the starting point would be domestic animals with which all pupils were familiar. Some pupils did recount occasions on which they had discussed what they learned at school with their families. Using examples from a context familiar to parents relieved a certain embarrassment that arose when parents realized that they could not understand curriculum topics which were quite new to them.

In Ethiopia and Sri Lanka, very practical, contextualised teaching approaches were observed. In one Sri Lankan school, pupils carried out practical activities in an experimental agricultural plot and these same activities were then used to help pupils learn mathematics concepts or to support English language teaching. In an Ethiopian school, pupils were also observed undertaking simple experiments using agricultural materials. Teachers stated that as a result of using the experimental plot, pupils' curiosity and questioning had increased, asking such questions as "How do we increase the yield of this crop?", "What new technologies can we use?"

In many cases, especially where the curriculum is centrally produced and flexibility is limited, teachers can at least make linkages between prescribed subjects and the agricultural environment. Where there is greater flexibility, teachers may be able to integrate different components of the curriculum and apply a topic-oriented approach by identifying with their students a project which is based on an agricultural theme.

Agriculture is only one aspect of the lives of rural people. It is not a source of income for everyone living in rural areas and it may be familiar as only one aspect of the environment. There are many contextual features which are familiar to everyone, however, such as nutrition and health. The natural (ecological) environment is clearly a resource for contextualisation. Just as agriculture can be used as a medium for contextualising learning across the curriculum, so can other aspects of life.

3.1.1.2. Teacher Training and Support

Such support can be provided through both pre-service and in-service training, but of course it depends upon the knowledge and capacity of the teacher trainers themselves to provide appropriate training. Thus, training of the trainers in innovative approaches will be necessary, as will awareness raising and training for educational administrators and school inspectors. There will also be a need for more of a 'training and coaching' approach to teachers' professional development, where teachers maintain a closer professional contact with their colleagues and their trainers, rather than undergoing very occasional, 'one-off' training events.

Generally speaking, teacher development will need to become a more participatory process than it has been traditionally. Teacher trainers (both initial and in-service), teachers and pupils need to become collaborative learners.

3.1.1.3. Building Partnerships and Co-operation

Partnerships between different organisations and institutions are vital. There is probably not one individual, group or organisation which has the capacity alone to bring about effective change in basic education. Synergies and complementarities must be sought. Many of the success stories presented here have involved partnerships between several quite different stakeholders. For example, a programme of change which requires teachers to introduce new methods of teaching and learning may well require curricular change. Change to the examination and assessment system is also likely to be needed, if success is to be attained.

Establishing this kind of co-operative arrangement is often difficult and may take time, however, a fact which needs to be appreciated more widely. Although participation is seen by many agencies as a 'good thing', the associated requirement for additional time and resources is not always recognised. Also, increasing the level of participation of different stakeholders inevitably leads to issues of power and conflicts between different groups and individuals.

In basic education, there are many marginalised groups: children from poor families, remote rural locations or with special needs; girls; women teachers, poor members of rural communities etc. It is also unrealistic to speak of 'rural communities', 'teachers', 'pupils' or 'parents' as homogeneous groups. Within such groups, very diverse interests are usually represented. Finding ways which allow real participation of groups such as these is very difficult.

3.1.1.4. Resource, Cost and Monitoring Issues

Although much attention is given by education funders to the economic basis for any educational reform, estimation of the returns for any educational investment is always complex. Educational cost-benefit analysis is notoriously difficult and is often controversial. Although it is certainly possible to consider budgets and expenditure from individual projects and then to try to extrapolate these to create figures for the cost of contextualised approaches, ultimately the resources required (and the costs) will be determined by the local context.

Teacher training and support will clearly require adequate funding. Funds will be required for investment in professional development of teachers, headteachers and teacher trainers. This will be needed not only for the actual initial training and on-going support and coaching, but also for the management of this staff development process, within the schools and also at a higher level, with the local education authorities, for example. Schools inspectors may also require awareness raising in new approaches and methodologies. In relation to this, resources will be needed for materials development. Some of this may be achieved locally, ideally within the schools themselves.

In practice, it is extremely important to advocate for a decentralised budget, covering staff development and also enabling teachers to prepare materials and to facilitate experiential learning through practical activities. This will have an implication also for physical resources. Although many schools will never be able to afford specialised classroom furniture, even individual chairs, at least the learning environment should be made safe and be kept at an ambient temperature. A minimum level of visual aids such as a blackboard and chalk or even home-made display equipment is obviously needed, but as learning becomes more active and participatory, then the requirement for suitable learning materials increases, as does the cost.

There is some advantage therefore in providing teachers with training in production of teaching and learning resources using locally available materials, being cheaper, repairable and replaceable if necessary. For institutionalising methods and approaches, the main issues were already raised above. Increased teacher participation in curriculum and learning strategy development will require resources for meetings and materials and more time from teachers. The reality of the lives of many teachers in rural schools is a combination of teaching and other work to ensure that they can support themselves and their families. The more time spent in the school which is not covered by their meagre salaries, the less time they have available for other forms of income-generation.

For this reason, many projects find it necessary to provide teachers with a financial incentive for the additional time they spend on project-related activities. Many pilot projects run successfully as long as external funding is available, but once this stops, the initiative rapidly draws to a close. It is worth reiterating the importance of ensuring financial support from the normal government institutional channels beyond the life of an externally funded project. This means that innovative approaches may need to be approved by the formal education system, a process that is often drawn-out and bureaucratic. For this reason, forward planning is essential and strategies for institutionalisation of innovations need to be considered at the start of projects rather than the end, to avoid financial crises which put an end to otherwise successful efforts.

Finally, most educational change takes much longer than many other development interventions and so it often takes longer to see the impact. This may be problematic for investors and donors in education who would like to see short-term benefits from their investments. For this reason, it is important that all stakeholders in education initiatives think early on about indicators of success, based on other experiences and on the reality of the local environment and are involved continuously and transparently in monitoring processes. Initially, the biggest gains are likely to be in human resource development, the results of which are often hard to measure quantitatively, but in the long term, this human capital will prove an essential resource for further improvement in the quality of teaching and learning.

3.1.1.5. Implications for Planning and Curriculum Issues

One of the most difficult issues to deal with is the dichotomy between the frequent requirement for a national, centralised curriculum with the need to create greater local, decentralised curricular adaptation. National planners will certainly continue to develop national curricula. The great challenge is to empower and enable teachers to interpret a prescribed curriculum in relation to a local context. In order to contextualise teaching and learning, a teacher must identify aspects of the learners' experience which will provide a valuable resource of basic concepts, metaphors and analogies to which the content of the curriculum can be related.

Such an approach has implications for teacher training and support.

Teachers would need to develop an understanding of local agricultural conditions and also to have the capacity to learn from the local environment and from their pupils. It would be necessary, also, for teachers to be able to produce learning materials which draw on agriculture as the context for the learning. Some school text books have been produced recently which encourage teachers to use agricultural illustrations for mathematics, science and languages.

Also a large amount of useful learning material relating to agriculture and sustainable rural development is now available in electronic form and can be found, for example, on the internet. The whole area of information communication technologies does of course have immense potential, but as yet, very few schools in remote rural areas have access to ICTs. Indeed, many do not even have supplies of electricity or telephones.

It is worth noting, however, that central nodes in education support systems, for example in provincial or district towns, will increasingly have access to ICTs. There may be great future potential in regional education advisers and teacher trainers downloading learning materials, or perhaps, the ideas behind those materials and disseminating them to primary school teachers who in turn can adapt them for local contextualisation. Building relationships between teachers and other local stakeholders, including of course the individual learners, is another key issue.

To enable teachers to achieve this, bearing in mind the heavy burdens they already carry, national planners will need to consider carefully the load of the curriculum itself and where possible to lighten it. If curricula are 'fixed but not full', teachers may be able to identify entry points through which they can build learning upon the local context. They may need help to do this, certainly, but without the space to manoeuvre, even well trained teachers will not be able to change the way in which they work. One practical strategy to help teachers manage the process of curriculum development and interpretation at school level is to institute regular 'curriculum conferences' which are empowering events involving teachers, school inspectors, tutors, etc.

3.2. Gardenbased Learning in Schools

Theoretical and methodological approaches to gardenbased learning vary greatly across the educational landscape, however the application of the pedagogy falls principally under one of two frameworks, experiential education (in contemporary language frequently referred to as projectbased learning) and/or environmental education. In theoretical terms gardenbased learning also finds relevance in two contemporary educational theories, Howard Gardner's theory on multiple intelligences and Daniel Goleman's theory of emotional intelligence.

3.2.1. Experiential Education and Projectbased Learning

There has been a significant growth in interest in experiential education and projectbased learning as educators recognise the value of hands-on learning. In its simplest form experiential education is best described by the American Association for Experiential Education, which states that "Experiential education is a process through which a learner constructs knowledge, skill and value from direct experiences." Projectbased learning (PBL) has been at the roots of effective education and was called for by early educational philosophers and practitioners.

Most PBL practitioners see this strategy as complementary to the formal curriculum and believe it is "not a separate subject, like mathematics: it provides a context for applying mathematical concepts and skills. Nor is project work an add-on to the basics; it should be treated as integral to all the other work included in the curriculum". While experiential education and projectbased learning offer excellent strategies or pedagogies, they require a contextual framework or thematic structure in which to operate. Environmental education and more specifically gardenbased learning can provide that context or thematic focus.

3.2.1.1. Philosophical roots of gardenbased instruction

The philosophical roots of gardenbased instruction can be found in the work of many educational theorists. The philosophies of Comenius, Rousseau, Pestalozzi, Froebel, Dewey, Montessori and Gardner all relate in some way to gardenbased learning. Here are just a few examples:

- *Comenius*: For every school "… there should be a garden attached where they (students) may feast their eyes on trees, flowers and plants … where they always hope to hear and see something new. Since the senses are the most trusty servants of the memory, this method (gardens) of sensuous perception will lead to the permanent retention of knowledge".
- *Rousseau*: "… since everything that enters into human understanding comes through the senses, the first reason of man is a reason of the senses. Our first masters of knowledge are our feet, our hands and our eyes".
- *Pestalozzi*: "Students observe first all of the objects in the classroom, observing and naming everything. When this is exhausted, they are taken into the garden, into the fields and woods - where they are led to notice objects in greater detail, their permanent and changeable qualities, the qualities that are general and those that are peculiar to them, their influence, their function, their destiny".
- *Froebel*: "The pupil will get the clearest insight into the character of things, of nature and surroundings, if he sees and studies them in their natural connection … the objects that are in closest and most constant connection with him, that owe their being to him … these are the things of his nearest surroundings … the garden, the farm, the meadow, the field, the forest, the plain… Instruction should proceed from the nearest and known to the less near and less known".
- *Dewey*: "Where schools are equipped with gardens … opportunities exist for reproducing situations of life and for acquiring and applying information and ideas in carrying forward of progressive experiences. Gardening need not be taught either for the sake of preparing future gardeners, or as an agreeable way of passing time. It affords an avenue of approach to knowledge of the place farming and horticulture have had in the history of the human race and which they occupy in present social organisation. Carried on in an environment educationally controlled, they (gardens) are means for making a study of the facts of growth, the chemistry of soil, the role of light, air,

moisture, injurious and helpful animal life, etc. There is nothing in the elementary study of botany, which cannot be introduced in a vital way in connection with caring for the growth of seeds. Instead of a subject belonging to a peculiar study called 'botany,' it will then belong to life and will find, moreover, its natural correlation with the facts of soil, animal life and human relations ... It is pertinent to note that in the history of man, the sciences grew gradually out of useful social occupations".

- *Montessori*: "When he (the student) knows that the life of the plants that have been sown depends upon his care in watering them ... without which the little plant dries up, ... the child becomes vigilant, as one who is beginning to feel a mission in life".
- *Gardner*: "Just as most ordinary children readily master language at an early age so too are most children predisposed to explore the world of nature".

It must be recognised that while all of the advice provided by these figures is relevant in gardenbased learning, a similar relationship can be drawn to other forms of experiential and/or environmental education. In the United States, the history of children's gardens and gardenbased learning is well documented from the 1890s to the present. The school garden history in other parts of the world and through earlier civilisations is less well documented.

In each era the lure of gardenbased learning in basic education was premised on its facilitation of the following educational strategies that are universally accepted as valid, if not essential, pedagogical approaches to meaningful learning. While certainly related, these concepts - learn-bydoing, projectbased learning, real world learning, child-centred learning -clearly focus on engaging the learner as the central figure in educational experience and in allowing individual and social constructivism. In addition, as Meyer states, school gardens were seen as settings that "create a sense of community, instil concern for the environment, foster a connection with nature and help students to develop self-confidence, discipline, skills in co-operation and multi-cultural understanding." In historical perspective we see that gardenbased learning is predicated as a contribution to all aspects of basic education:

- academic skills;
- personal development;
- social development;
- moral development;
- vocational and/or subsistence skills;
- life skills.

3.2.2. Future Directions

The gardenbased learning programmes in developed and developing countries show many similarities in basic motivations for using the garden. In virtually all settings the garden is viewed as a tool of multiple uses:

- to support core academic training, particularly in science and math;
- to add a sense of excitement, adventure, emotional impact and aesthetic appreciation to learning;
- to teach basic skills and vocational competencies;
- to teach about food and fibre production;
- to teach ecological literacy and/or environmental education;
- to teach sustainable development;
- to produce food and other commodities for subsistence consumption and trade;
- to improve nutrition, diet and health;
- to teach the art and science of cooking with fresh products from the garden or local farms;
- to re-establish the celebratory nature of a shared meal.

There is a difference in the degree to which developed and developing countries emphasize various elements in the garden mission or objectives, however the differences are not as pronounced as was expected. In considering best practices for gardenbased learning, the first and possibly most important is the establishment of a sound rationale or framework for the pedagogy. A second critical area for consideration involves questions on how to start and sustain a programme in gardenbased learning.

3.2.2.1. *Educational integrity*

In the developed economies, gardenbased learning is viewed by some as a more effective strategy for basic education. However, to accept this idea requires a general improvement of the educational integrity of the practice. There is a need for an overall educational strategy statement and implementation guide for gardenbased learning that articulates the advantages of the pedagogy and makes the connection between the practice and various proposals for educational reform (experiential education, emotional intelligence, etc.). Such guidelines exist for environmental education and agricultural education and could serve as a template for gardenbased learning. A strong emphasis on improved academic performance in schools within some countries has meant that gardenbased learning must be tied to the standards and benchmarks in core subjects to attain credibility within the educational community. There is a large body of knowledge that suggests that science education can be improved though use of an applied, hands-on curriculum.

3.2.2.2. *Garden maintenance*

For schools and programmes with a significant investment in garden infrastructure (physical site, equipment, plant material, etc.) there is a growing realisation that a garden co-ordinator or strategic plan (e.g., Garden of Learning) must be in place to effectively engage these resources as educational tools. Relying on overworked teachers, custodians, groundskeepers or transient volunteers is not a sustainable strategy. The garden must be viewed as an integral part of the educational plan for the school (e.g., as a classroom) and financed accordingly as a part of the overhead of operations. If this is not the case, then long-term sustainability is in jeopardy and the garden becomes a burden to the creative energies of staff, parents and community volunteers.

3.2.2.3. *Educational linkages*

School gardens and gardenbased learning in some settings seem to lead to a new sense of community at the school. This encourages greater participation by parents and community members, not unlike athletics, but perhaps in a more nurturing, less competitive environment.

3.2.2.4. *International linkages*

Many gardens are used to grow the traditional food of a variety of cultures. This emphasis on cultural diversity has led a number of programmes to establish international linkages for exchange of ideas, seeds and, hopefully, students. There are exciting opportunities for the established school gardens of the developed economies to partner with the developing world school gardens to support their growth.

References

Bude, U. (Ed.), *Culture and environment in primary education,* Bonn: DSE, ZED, 1993.

Riedmiller, S., "Primary school agriculture - What can it realistically achieve?" In: *Entwicklung Landlicher Raum* (3), 1994..

Taylor, P.; Mulhall, A., *Contextualizing teaching and learning in rural primary schools: using agricultural experience,* Vol. I. London: DFID, 1997.

Tuan, Y., "Children and the natural environment", In: Altman, I. and Wohlwill, J.F., (Eds), *Children and the Environment.* New York: Plenium Press, 1978.

Van Lierop, P., "Ecology education in primary schools", In: *ILEIA Newsletter,* 1997.

4

Rural Skills Development

Rural people in general are the most disadvantaged in terms of access to services, including education and training, and are the worst served by infrastructure of various kinds. Rural people are most likely in many settings to be amongst those who are not being reached in the drive towards the Millennium Development Goals (MDGs). Moreover, such problems are typically starker for rural women and girls, given their multiple burdens. In spite of the pro-poor orientation of much of international and national development policy for more than a decade, there are ways in which the situation of rural areas has got worse. In some cases, rural areas are the most adversely affected by HIV/AIDS. Their historical brain drain to the cities has been accelerated by the international outflow of skilled people from poorer countries.

Rural location does much to increase several of these problems. Moreover, the location of many public providers under Ministries of Agriculture is widely held to exacerbate the problem by making agricultural education and training a backwater that is largely cut off from the transformation processes being experienced in systems led by Ministries of Education or Labour.

4.1. Contribution of Skills Development for Rural People to the MDGs

One of the strongest reasons for a focus on skills development for rural people is that 70 percent of the world poor are rural. Skills development is essential to consolidate agriculture, and by strengthening the agriculture sector, progress will be made towards achieving the MDGs. The following points show the potentially positive relationship between education and skills, agriculture and rural development, and the MDGs:

4.1.1. MDG 1: Eradicate Extreme Poverty and Hunger

Much of poverty and hunger is concentrated in rural areas. There is also strong evidence for the direct impact of literacy rates on hunger and poverty. Agricultural production stimulates employment and improves incomes. At the same time, food security positively affects labour productivity, livelihoods and education. Thus, there is the possibility of a virtuous cycle between food security, sustainable agriculture and education and training.

4.1.2. MDG 2: Achieve universal Primary Education

There is a clear effect of illiteracy on poverty, food security and nutrition and vice versa. Hunger, malnutrition and food insecurity erode cognitive abilities and reduce school attendance. Conversely, illiteracy and lack of education reduce earning capacity, and contribute directly to hunger and poverty.

4.1.3. MDG 3: Promote Gender Equality and Empower Women

Women's role in agriculture, access to resources and skills is of great importance. Moreover, the education of girls has positive effects on family' health, productivity and well being. The gender gap is usually more pronounced in rural areas.

4.1.4. MDG 4: Reduce Child Mortality

There is a clear negative effect of hunger, malnutrition and lack of micronutrients on child health and mortality.

4.1.5. MDG 5: Improve Maternal Health

Improved education, the introduction of labour-saving technologies and better nutrition can all significantly improve maternal health.

4.1.6. MDG 6: Combat HIV/AIDS, Malaria and Other Diseases

Improvements in both education and nutrition can reduce the incidence of such diseases and resistance to them. The protection of forests can also contribute as they provide a vital source of medicinal plants.

4.1.7. MDG 7: Promote Environmental Sustainability

This can be promoted through ecologically sustainable management of agriculture and natural resources. Moreover, it is clear that hunger and poverty compel over-exploitation of natural resources thus compromising environmental sustainability.

4.1.8. MDG 8: Develop a Global Partnership for Development

A cross-sectoral focus such as that of education for rural development necessarily promotes the multi-agency mobilisation of resources for achievement of the MDGs.

4.2. Potential of Agricultural Systems

For the rural economy, developments in the agricultural system bring food, jobs, incomes and services for rural people. For the national economy, such improvements bring food for urban people, public revenue, skilled labour for other sectors, foreign exchange, jobs, income and investment.

4.2.1. Major Farming Systems Deserve Greater Attention

There needs to be greater attention paid to the major farming systems: Maize Mixed, Cereal-Root Crop, Root Crop, Forest-based and Pastoral.

4.2.2. Major Challenge of Smallholders

Smallholders represent the vast majority of farmers in developing countries. Their inherent strengths include their ability to make effective decisions, manage labour efficiently, optimise land productivity and adopt new technology. However, their competitiveness is constrained in globalised markets with stringent standards and unfair trade. Moreover, they face constraints of services, investment, technology, etc.

4.2.3. Sustainable Agriculture and Rural Development

The FAO/UNESCO partnership is rooted in the notion of sustainable development and the crucial role that agriculture and rural development play in such framework. This had its origins in the Earth Summit (Rio) and was given further impetus by the Sustainable Development Summit (Johannesburg).

The approach is centred on people's livelihoods: what they have, they know, they want and they can do. The approach is beneficial because it seeks to relate this livelihoods focus to a range of factors and contexts. In particular, it considers the cultural, social, economic and environmental dimensions. It focuses on agriculture, rural enterprises and the linkages between them. It considers policy, institutions, technology and investment.

Success stories for this approach at national level indicate a range of important issues. First, there is a clear pay-off for having a long term vision, clear strategy and priority on development of agriculture and the rural sector. Second, there are good returns on investment in human capital and key institutions for sustainable rural development. Third, similar benefits can be had from investment in rural infrastructure (roads, health, education, communication, etc.). Fourth, the approach provides an effective strategy for coordinating and working with international community.

4.2.4. Participatory Monitoring and Evaluation Systems

This approach stresses the importance of participatory monitoring and evaluation systems (PM&E). These are designed to learn what works, to draw lessons and to share innovations. Moreover, they engender real participation of local communities and households. PM&E is an essential tool for using resources efficiently, leveraging collaboration and mobilising resources from all stakeholders. PM&E encourages strengthening institutional and community capacities. It leads to the development of indicators that are meaningful to local people and using the information generated to assess policies, institutions and programmes. However, there is a tendency in some projects to use the language of PM&E because the donors like it rather than really because there is a concern with local empowerment and democracy.

4.2.5. Agricultural Education and Training

Conventional agricultural education and training (AET) has tended to have an excessive focus on public sector jobs and on-farm employment. There has been a lack of consideration for new skill areas, such as environment and natural resource management, biotechnology, agribusiness, etc. Delivery has been fragmented, with a lack of clear learning pathways. There has been a growing lack of relationships between providers and the labour market as the latter diversifies. There has been an excessive focus on tertiary level qualifications but a weak articulation between research and training. Enrolment capacity remains low.

4.3. Rationale for Rural Skills Development

Rural skills development is a necessary priority for a number of reasons. In Sub-Saharan Africa in particular, the food security challenge leads to an urgent need to increase productivity. Skills will be important here. Globally, the environmental challenge leads to the need for better skills for protecting the environment. An economic challenge highlights the importance of skills that can contribute to economic growth and the international competitiveness of the agricultural sector. There is also a social challenge of skills development for poverty reduction, employment generation and social capital creation.

4.3.1. Education for Rural People Flagship

The ERP is a partnership launched at the Johannesburg Summit that bridges the agriculture and education sectors and the concerns of the World Food Summit and the Education for All initiative. It is conceived of in the spirit of MDG 8.

The ERP seeks to strengthen the capacity of Ministries of Education and Agriculture to

- Formulate adequate policies to address education needs of rural poor
- Improve quality and relevance of curriculum
- Ensure full participation of NGOs and private sector
- Mobilise donor support

The ERP partnership has led to new alliances among more than 200 partners including governments, agencies and civil society organisations. It has been integrated into national rural development and EFA policies in several countries including Kosovo, China, Venezuela and Mozambique. Capacity has been built nationally, regionally and internationally.

4.4. Transformation of Rural Labour Markets

Globalisation is having a powerful impact of on rural labour markets. There has been a strong rise in non-farm employment and income in many rural areas. This has been accompanied by a diversification of employment patterns.

4.4.1. Rise of Non-farm Employment

In most developed countries farm employment has been decreasing significantly over the years. The current trend is towards a rise in labour productivity, contributing to a decline in agricultural employment. Furthermore, an increasing proportion of farm work is delegated to farm workers.

In OECD countries the number of farms has declined and the volume of labour allocated to farming has dropped significantly. In developing countries, the employment changes in the agriculture sector vary greatly, but in the long run, the capacity of agriculture to absorb labour surpluses is questionable. While in many countries, technological innovation is contributing to employment reduction in agriculture, many developing countries are not able to absorb the released workforce.

The transformation of rural labour markets has much to do with domestic and external macroeconomic pressures. In the context of globalisation, the degree of vulnerability of agriculture and therefore of rural labour markets to international economic change is greater. In Mexico, for instance, trade liberalisation associated with the removal of subsidies to agriculture had a significant impact on labour-migration, rural workers migrating to urban areas or to the US.

However, macroeconomic developments influence farm households not only by affecting prices of agricultural commodities but by affecting employment opportunities in the non-farm sector. As a general trend, there is a greater prevalence of non-farm employment and pluri-activity among farm households and a correspondingly greater dependence on non-farm income. Traditionally, agriculture has been considered as the main sector for employment creation in rural areas. Hence, for many people, 'rural' and 'agriculture' are synonymous. Increasingly, policy makers realise that the job creation potential of the farm sector is limited and that new sources of rural employment will be required in the future.

It is estimated that in sub-Saharan Africa and Latin America about 40 to 45 per cent of average rural household income originates from non-farm activities. This share already represents around 30 to 40 per cent in South Asia. In Bangladesh, a country where about 80 per cent of the population is rural, the relative size of the rural non-farm sector in the labour market is quite substantial and has been growing. Similarly, the country experienced a corresponding increase in rural non-farm income. Further development of the non-farm rural activities is seen as an important strategy to reduce the incidence of rural poverty.

Although the rise of the non-farm rural economy seems to be a global trend, the nature of the activities involved vary greatly from country to country, depending on the level of development. In sub-Saharan Africa and South Asia, where rural poverty is widely spread, non-farm activities remain closely linked to agriculture and poorly related to the urban economy. Depending on the specificities of each zone, there is a tendency, notably in the poorest areas, to derive non-farm income from migration to cities or abroad.

In Latin America, where the rural people represents a lower share of the total population, light manufacturing is growing in rural areas within the framework of increasing urban/rural economic linkages. This pattern is even more prominent in East and South East Asia where the rural non-farm economy combines various types of agriculture related activities with more advanced forms of manufacturing. Gender can also be an important determinant to analyse the rise of non-farm rural employment.

On the contrary agriculture remained the major source of employment for rural men, with the sole exception of Costa Rica. The effects of trade liberalisation, agriculture policy reform and technological change on rural labour markets are also very different in rural areas with access to off-farm job opportunities and in remote rural regions. In poor rural areas with easy access to urban centres, it is expected that labour supplied by farm households to urban labour markets will increase.

These trends are related to changes in technology, in the demographic composition of farm households and in the relative economic return to farm labour. Typically, labour supply is influenced by several factors such as age, gender and education. Age and education are found to be among the most important determinants of off-farm work. The increasing educational attainment levels in rural areas can influence the allocation of labour resources. A higher level of education increases the endowment of human capital and therefore opens access to higher non-farm wages.

In OECD countries, higher average education levels of farm women contributed to increasing female off-farm work. In fact, increasing the level of education in the agriculture sector can produce opposite results on employment strategies. It is generally accepted that more education allows farmers to access and process information, allocate resources and adopt new technologies more effectively. By raising the farm earning capacity, this would suggest that education reduces farm exits.

Schooling also increases the opportunity for employment outside the sector and thus reduces the capacity of the agriculture sector to retain the most educated components of the workforce. The distinction between specific and general education can clarify this relationship. While farm-specific training is likely to contribute to retain labour force in the agriculture sector, more general types of education may increase the probability of leaving the sector for non-farm employment.

In a process of rural transformation, higher levels of education among the farm population and the availability of off-farm jobs facilitate the adjustment. A major concern is that non-farm activities can be difficult to access for the rural poor, partly due to their low level of education and training. Hence, education should be an entire part of support interventions aiming at developing economic activities beyond agriculture in rural areas.

Implications of the transformation of rural labour markets for skill development are critical since training for agriculture, as an explicit goal, is increasingly challenged by the need to prepare for non-farm employment as well as for coping strategies in a rapidly changing environment. However, the provision of technical skills is often not prepared to address the needs of rural labour markets. Besides the trend towards industry specialisation, in many countries rural areas become the host of new forms of tourism.

In recent years increasing attention has being paid to pro-poor tourism initiatives. Among the factors that influence the benefits to the poor from tourism, skills constitute a key determinant. Therefore, targeted education and training programmes form an important component of strategies to enhance the economic participation of the poor in tourism enterprise.

4.4.2. Technical and Vocational Education and Training in Rural Areas

The transformation of rural labour markets implies that delivery systems should be relevant to the needs of rural people engaged in a wide range of economic activities including agriculture but also industrial activities, tourism and other services. The term agricultural education and training (AET) system to describe the various delivery structures providing skills for agriculture and rural development.

Skills for rural labour markets are offered by a great diversity of public and private providers. Within the public sector, institutions are in most cases affiliated to various ministries and government agencies, often without clear overall coordination. For this reasons, the term AET system is not used here. This semantic choice is also consistent with the rise of non-farm employment and therefore the need to expand the traditional concept of agricultural education to a broader approach of skills for rural development. In most developing countries agricultural education has been attracting critics. Excessive focus on public sector jobs and on farm employment, lack of consideration for new areas such as environment and natural resources management, biotechnology or agribusiness are some of the limitations often mentioned.

The rehabilitation of skills provision for rural areas can find useful resources in the broader debate on technical and vocational education and training. In fact many of the rigidities that constrain training in agriculture are also present in the broader technical and vocational education system. Beyond agriculture and rural development, training policies are considered critical to meet the challenges of knowledge- and skills-based societies.

Globalisation and the need to maintain, through skill development, international competitiveness appear as the strongest force. Associated with globalisation is the deep transformation of labour markets, including in rural areas and the need to adjust training systems and policies accordingly. Today the reforms introduced in technical and vocational education and training already contribute to a renewal of skill development concepts and approaches for rural areas. To some extent the innovations introduced in agricultural education have sometimes also contributed to inspire broader training reforms.

The rapid and deep transformation of jobs and skills is probably the most powerful motivation to change training provision. A lot of attention has been given to the occupational transformation in industry, as a result of both changing work organisation and new technologies. Yet, this process also affects the agriculture sector as reflected in the case of technical foresters.

Renewing modes of delivery has also been a major challenge for training reform. In this respect a central concern is to consolidate linkages between employers and providers. It is worth noting that rural trainers have had a long experience in this field. The main objective of these institutions was to train farmers that would stay in their community and continue to work on the family farm.

Through various modalities, including apprenticeship, linking education and work experience constitutes today, beyond the agriculture sector, a major component of most vocational education reforms. Finding better ways, besides formal provision, of combating poverty is a highest priority in many countries. Designing community-based responses, linking training provision to basic needs and to local development initiatives constitutes a much needed approach in rural areas.

One promising example in relation to poverty alleviation and employment promotion is the vocational training programme for youth employment which was implemented in collaboration with ILO, through a technical co-operation project (POCET) in Honduras. This initiative resulted in an improved level of income-generating activities for young people in covered rural areas.

Beyond the contribution of training to poverty reduction through community linkages, the response of technical and vocational education to social and economic change requires creating new forms of co-operation and partnership with the labour market. In addition to macro-level policy initiatives to cross traditional borders of responsibilities between stakeholders, a major challenge lies with the motivation and capacity of institutions to enter new fields. If traditional vocational schools are mainly concerned with delivery, they increasingly need to engage in various forms of collaboration with employers to provide company-based training and job placement services to students and also to offer continuing education and other types of support to enterprises.

Financing is obviously a critical dimension of any policy for skill development in rural areas. Exploring new financing arrangements for skills development is often seen as an imperative because governments are not able, or not prepared, to provide all the additional resources required to expand and improve the national skills base. According to the economic rationale, those who benefit from training should pay for it.

In many countries, pre-employment, initial and institutionbased training is still considered to be a government responsibility, while financing of continuing training and education is left to the social partners. In reality policies are trapped in a situation where extra resources are needed but public expenditure is restricted. In most developing countries, governments are unable to provide the required resources for skills development. Moreover, in the post-Dakar Education for All framework, government resources for education are directed on priority to basic education.

Increasingly, funding for vocational education and training is based on tripartite mechanisms, which include government, individuals and employers. In countries where decentralisation processes are progressing, local governments are providing resources for training and skills development. By and large, governments retain primary responsibility to promote and co-finance skills development. Frequently this includes creating incentives for employers and for individuals to invest more in skills development. The current trend emphasises the role of employers and individuals in contributing to the costs of skills development. The concept of funding partnerships illustrates this approach. It is often concretised by the establishment of training funds typically funded by a payroll tax.

It is important to stress the fact that this trend towards increasing employers' contributions is not purely a financial issue. The aim is not only to mobilise additional resources, but also to increase the overall involvement of employers in steering and delivery mechanisms for training. Such an increased involvement is expected to improve the quality of training delivery and to align training supply with the requirements of employment. Hence, financing of skills development is very much linked to the issues of responsiveness to market needs, to adaptation and relevance of training. Besides concerns of relevance and effectiveness, alleviating poverty requires that more money be spent in favour of the most vulnerable groups of the population, often located in rural areas, where the experience shows that the private sector is poorly interested in investing. On grounds of equity, there is a strong case to redirect expenditures where social problems are the most difficult. More creativity is also required to design innovative funding schemes for financing, in a sustainable way, access to training for the poor.

4.5. Rural Skills Development: Future Trends and Experiences

The diversity of countries, labour markets and education and training systems in Asia makes it difficult to draw a general pattern. Although the regional trend reflects a decline in terms of employment generation in agriculture, the sector remains, in most cases, a major contributor to GDP formation and job provision. In recent years, the deterioration of the unemployment and underemployment situation in agriculture and a decline in the productivity of the sector, have constituted a major concern in many countries of the region.

China illustrates both the massive need for upgrading the skills of the population in rural areas and the challenge of developing alternative patterns of labour market transition for the huge labour force leaving the agriculture sector. In China, the rural population still occupies about 70 per cent of the national total. Among the total rural labour force, approximately 275 million people are engaged in farming. Only 3.4 per cent received primary school education and 0.13 per cent received vocational education. There are only about 20 per cent of farmers who have received short-term training on practical technology and on average, the number of agricultural technicians is not sufficient to provide adequate support to farmers.

At the higher education level almost 60 per cent of income is derived from activities in industry. These results reflect the diversification of economic activities in rural China. They also show that households with low education backgrounds are at a disadvantage to seize the new opportunities offered due to the transformation of the rural economy.

While vocational education and training are most needed, they are also the weakest in poor rural areas. Addressing the needs of the rural poor faces three major challenges. First, in poor remote areas, traditions often provide a resistance to a change in production modes through the introduction of new knowledge and skills. Fostering the demand for training requires offering concrete success stories to which local people can relate.

Second, while the overall education profile of rural areas has increased significantly in recent years, the disparities among regions have also widened. Third, the perceived need for 'breaking away from farming' in poor rural areas resulted in much attention being paid to the development of primary and middle school education with the intention of increasing the transition to higher education. In this process the need to improve the labour market relevance of vocational education and training was overlooked.

The first level of vocational education is provided at the junior secondary level, part of the 9-year compulsory education. At the senior secondary level technical and vocational education is provided by four different types of institutions geared towards various types of skills.

In addition to its small capacity, vocational education in poor areas suffers from low levels of teacher qualification plus the lack of training facilities in order to give students exposure to real working conditions. In fact, attending higher educational institutions is often seen as the main aim of vocational education. As a result it is disconnected from local labour markets.

Within the framework of the development of the nine-year compulsory education, the expansion of vocational education was accelerated at the junior, middle and senior levels with middle schools being the main component. In addition, large-scale training programmes on agricultural skills, science and technology are conducted for farmers and rural workers in an effort to foster local development. Beyond quantitative expansion, the new attention being paid to vocational education and training reflects a broader strategy to adjust human resources to industrial restructuring in both rural and urban areas. This adjustment is part of the broad shift from a socialist to a market-oriented economy.

In India formal education in agriculture is about a century old. Towards the last quarter of nineteenth Century a few institutions were set up in different parts of India to offer certificate, diploma or licence courses in agriculture. Agricultural education started with the setting up of five agricultural colleges. These colleges were established at Lyalpur, Pune, Coimbatore, Sabour and Kempur on the recommendations of the Famine Commission of 1901.

Agricultural education contributed to the response to the challenges posed by extreme vagaries of nature and to turn an extreme food shortage economy into a food surplus economy. Hence, besides research, agricultural education made it possible to evolve such varieties that are resistant to pest and diseases and also develop new techniques of crop cultivation in the drought-affected areas.

There are many constraints on agriculture in India that pose challenges to agricultural education, extension and research. This is reflected by the fact that the average yield is much less in India than in many countries. As in other countries, increasing productivity is one of the objectives of agricultural vocational education.

References

Bennell, P., "Learning to change: skills development among the economically vulnerable and socially excluded in developing countries", In: *Employment and Training Papers,* Geneva: ILO, 1999.

FAO, *Report of the expert consultation on strategy options for higher education in agriculture,* Rome, Italy, Rome: FAO, 16-20 December 1991.

________________, *Training for agriculture and rural development 1995-96,* Rome: FAO, 1996.

5

Higher Education and Rural Development

5.1. Higher Agricultural Education

Higher agricultural education evolved to educate the professional and technical human resources needed to push the frontiers of technology for agriculture. This was achieved by graduating degree holders with bachelors, masters and doctorates for careers largely related to production agriculture. Higher agricultural education has always been science based and many degrees were classified as "agricultural science".

Typically the programmes focused on natural sciences and mathematics, agriculture and varying amounts of social science. These were variously linked to research and production techniques that may, at various times, have included farm management, conservation agriculture, marketing and economics to produce graduates suitable for employment in research or extension in the public sector; production agriculture on family farms, as farm managers or in agribusiness with the private sector.

HAE, as part of higher education, is the provider of third level agricultural education. It can be located in agricultural universities or in colleges or departments of agriculture in the wider university; diplomagranting (sometimes third level sub degree) institutes or polytechnics, short term—one- or two-year diploma or certificate courses that prepare technicians for entry level extension work or entry level technician work with the public or private sector, in-service training programmes for extension staff, farmer training of short duration, adult training and young farmer education and training.

Typically, HAE is managed by ministries of education (MOE) and fits into the education system; sub-degree tertiary entities may be under the management of the MOE or the ministry of agriculture (MOA) and the diploma and certificate granting courses are usually under the supervision of the MOA.

Separate oversight and management divides rather than unites the various education and training programmes and very few examples exist where bridging can be made between levels. For example, an extension worker with secondary education and a two year agriculture certificate plus considerable field experience can rarely bridge to a degree programme.

HAE, in common with higher education in general, has its problems. Many of the problems in their most obvious state can be found in developing countries but similar problems manifest themselves in various degrees in the more developed countries as well. Few HAE entities suffer from all of the problems listed at any one time but there are some common themes that provide a generic pattern across the HAE landscape:

- National support for agricultural education has weakened;
- Investment in agricultural education by governments, donor agencies and organisations has dropped dramatically from the highs of the 1960s and 1970s;
- Funding is inadequate to maintain physical facilities and support minimum standards;
- The combination of lower investment and support has contributed to a qualitative decline in many agricultural education and training systems;
- Teaching and research standards have dropped;
- Insufficient practical and job-related skills are taught;
- Political interference prevents rationalisation of undergraduate and trainee intake, leading to overcrowding, decreasing per capita funding support, and low staff morale;
- Isolation has encouraged inbreeding in staff appointments;
- Agricultural education has tended to become isolated from mainstream academia;

- Curricula do not keep pace with changes in the sector and employer expectations;
- Unemployment of graduates, especially at tertiary level, is high;
- There is a change in the profile of students' backgrounds from mostly rural to increasingly urban;
- Programmes no longer attract the highest achievers from secondary streams;
- Information technology is underutilised.

5.1.1. Transforming HAE

The era of concern with production agriculture was a golden one for investment in HAE and, in a sense, a dangerous one institutionally for it created an illusion of an ever growing need for graduates of a certain profile entering a buoyant market anchored by the public sector. Donors were generous with support and production agriculture reacted positively to a combination of science, investment and education with dramatic productivity gains registered in many parts of the globe. In too many instances complacency set in.

High input-high output production agriculture, despite its success in defeating the spectre of mass hunger and famine, began to have negative impacts on the environment and increasing demands for natural resources, especially forests and water, raised questions about the planet's capacity to continue to support a growing and resource-hungry population.

The era of environmental conservation and natural resources management (NRM) was born. Many HAE entities were slow in reacting to this new concern and a large amount of the funding made available by donors and international organisations found its way to other parts of the education system. While many HAE institutions are struggling with survival and with catching up to the NRM/Environment movement a new challenge has emerged namely, that of rural development (RD).

Those advocating change in agricultural education are unanimous in their observation that HAE must go beyond a focus on production agriculture. This, despite the concern of many in HAE institutions, does not mean the end of agricultural education but it does mean that agricultural education will have to reinvent itself and be seen as part of a larger education concern for rural development and food security. Despite visible successes in producing more food, scientists are concerned about stagnation of yield growth rates and yield declines and the unpredictability of climate change and environmental degradation.

There are very few problems in today's world that can be solved by knowledge from only one discipline. The challenge is to have strong disciplinary departments, while at the same time engaging them in collaborative endeavours. Added most often are the non-teaching aspects of knowledge generation and dissemination (research and extension) needed in the service of society for the solution of its problems, first the domestic ones and then those reflecting the interdependence of the modern world. Another clue to the changing nature of the world's agricultural institutions is the operational conception of 'agriculture' making it more inclusive, reflecting the use of off-farm resources on food and fibre production systems, consumer concerns about quality and cost and the skills and technologies that integrate the physical farming part of the food chain with all the postharvest human uses and impact.

If higher agricultural education is to play an active and constructive role in rural development it will have to adjust its programmes to new and nontraditional topics, new teaching and learning models, new partnerships with academia, research organisations and rural space stakeholders, expanded representation in governance and continuous dialogue with policy-makers. Some of the realities that have to be addressed by HAE will include:

- Curriculum to be based on labour market surveys;
- Stakeholders must have input to HAE decision-making;
- Intakes (and outputs) must reflect both sector and rural space development needs;
- Incentives for teaching quality in place;
- Faculty members need to reflect a diversity of backgrounds and experiences;
- Closer ties with the wider education system;

- Team teaching within HAE disciplines and with HE system;
- Rural development practitioners as members of teaching teams;
- Researchers used as teaching resource;
- Practical work by students on university farms and in communities, including decision-making experience;
- Student attachment to rural enterprises including communities, farms and agribusinesses;
- Student evaluation of programmes' needs to be introduced;
- Co-operation with and inputs supplied to basic and secondary education;
- Focus on non-formal adult education and training programmes;
- Partnerships with other sector ministries and concerned stakeholders in the public and private sectors and with society at large;
- Research and analysis of decentralised government needs and provision of services;
- Policy advice to government;
- Staff training provided as contribution to morale and to education quality;
- Visiting scholars—teachers and researchers encouraged;
- Increased use of information technology;
- Greater stakeholder representation in HAE governance.

If HAE is to make a meaningful contribution to the process of rural development it must first understand the scope of that process and analyse the educational needs of stakeholders. Rural development has three important features with substantial implications for how rural development programmes are designed and implemented:

- Improving the living standards of the subsistence population involves mobilisation and allocation of resources so as to reach a desirable balance over time between welfare and productive services available to the subsistence rural sector.

- Mass participation requires that resources be allocated to low-income regions and classes and that the productive and social services actually reach them.
- Making the process self-sustaining requires development of the appropriate skills and implementing capacity and the presence of institutions at the local, regional and national levels to ensure the effective use of existing resources and to foster the mobilisation of additional financial and human resources for continued development of the subsistence sector. Self-sustenance thus means involving, as distinct from simply reaching, the subsistence populations through development programmes.

For this to happen, people must develop new ideas about themselves and the world around them, new attitudes and new hope for the future. This kind of transformation of the individual is essentially what education for rural development is all about. In contrast to the conventional notion that equates education with schooling, education should be equated with learning as a lifelong process involving a great variety of experiences.

However, to shift from the narrow school view of education to this wide lifelong view requires a change of focus that is extremely difficult for anyone whose thinking has been conditioned by very traditional formal education programmes. In addition, HAE's contribution to true rural development must also include involvement and support for the broader education for rural development that encompasses basic, secondary, vocational and adult education provided for all people in the rural space.

There are two critical areas where change can be initiated and supported. First, there must be national policy on HAE and indeed on education for rural development in general. These policies dealing with HAE need to be connected with the ones on education for rural development within the wider education policy rather than with the established and 'traditional' agricultural education and 'rural education' that are seen to be wanting. Second, HAE institutions themselves must be committed to catalysing change. Indeed HAE institutions must be able to advise and guide policy-makers on the problems and solutions to the provision of education and training for agriculture and rural development.

Experience shows that change will never take place if HAE institutions fail to take the initiative. Leadership is critical in bringing about change. Someone or some group needs to enable the institution to vision a future. The higher education change principles amongst which are:

- In order to change an institution, you must start everywhere at once. In changing a higher education system you must address structural issues, curricula, resource allocation, access, collaboration, technology and other variables that will influence the change you desire;
- Change must be value based and vision driven. Vision and values must be determined in collaboration with the stakeholders and the vision must be that of a preferred vision, not just trend driven. Being value based and vision driven is even more essential in times of rapidly changing systems that come about during periods of technological innovation and revolution;
- There must be a critical mass (but not necessarily a majority) for change to occur. A good example of this can be found in the example of the University of Cordoba in Spain where a dedicated group of faculty working inside the organisation and with external stakeholders managed to convince the university to launch a professional rural development programme in 1995;
- Change must occur within the resource structure of the institution—not just from philanthropic funds;
- For institutional change to occur, policy must be impacted, capacity built and budgets reallocated to new and more relevant programmes;
- There is strength and power in collaborations and partnerships that allow complementary solution finding rather than competition for scarce resources.

5.1.2. Desirable Features of Higher Education

Recent thinking about higher education in developing countries and about education sector strategies has much relevance for policy-makers who have the responsibility for ensuring that education for rural development has the vision, strategy and implementation resources necessary to make an impact on revitalising the rural space. The Task Force on Higher Education and Society presents nine desirable features of a higher education system all of which apply to HAE. These are:

5.1.2.1. *Stratified Structure*

Higher education is under great pressure to improve the quality of the education they offer—but also to educate increasing numbers of students. A stratified higher education is a hybrid that marries the goals of excellence and mass education, allowing each to be achieved within one system and using limited resources. A stratified higher education comprises one tier that is oriented towards research and selectivity and another that imparts knowledge to large numbers of students. Successful HAE entities enrich teaching and learning programmes by incorporating the findings of research.

5.1.2.2. *Adequate and Stable Long-term Funding*

Higher education institutions can thrive only if their funding levels are adequate, stable and, subject to good performance, secure in the long term. In many areas insecure funding stifles the ability and the incentive to carry out research. Governments have a crucial role to play in providing stability.

5.1.2.3. *Competition*

Traditionally there has been little competition within higher education systems. Competition is exceedingly difficult to achieve through central decree, but requires a high degree of autonomy for academic institutions, allowing them to exploit their strengths and overcome weaknesses. One common indicator of competition is faculty mobility between institutions, which tends to promote a healthy academic environment through intellectual cross-fertilisation. Declining standards of teaching and research in HAE can be attributed in part to its isolation from competition.

5.1.2.4. *Flexibility*

Higher education institutions need to be flexible if they are to be most effective. They need to be able to adapt quickly to changing enrolment levels, to the rise and fall of different fields of study and to changes in the mix of skills demanded in the labour market. Open institutions are more likely to keep pace with significant external changes. Scholarly interaction within and between countries, frequent curriculum review and strong connections to the world stock of knowledge (through substantial investments in Internet access, for example) are all important.

5.1.2.5. Well-defined Standards

Effective higher education institutions articulate clear standards and set for themselves challenging goals that are consistent with the needs of their societies and labour forces. International standards are especially relevant in a globalised economy. Some standards are needed for degree requirements when it comes to student performance, faculty qualifications and achievement. A culture of accountability is also essential, allowing improvement (or deterioration) to be continually monitored and rewarded.

5.1.2.6. Immunity from Political Manipulation

Higher education institutions are effective only when insulated from the undue influence of political parties, governments or short-term political developments in educational affairs. Excluding partisan political interests from the operation of a higher education institution helps to safeguard merit-based decision-making, one hallmark of an effective higher education institution. Political pressure to expand enrolment has been an unfortunate feature of HAE in recent times and has led to a lowering of standards of education and facilities.

5.1.2.7. Well-defined Links to Other Sectors

Higher education does not operate in isolation. It must pay attention to secondary education provision in order to take account of student preparation. It will also benefit primary and secondary education through training qualified teachers and demonstrating potential educational innovations.

Quality higher education will also increase students' aspirations at the primary and secondary levels, leading to higher standards as students compete for tertiary education places. Strong links between higher education and its environment can generate many beneficial effects, including significantly augmenting the resources available, helping to overcome intellectual isolation and allowing the achievement of 'critical mass' in a larger number of specialised fields. For example, advocates for higher education and industry can work together to ensure that graduates have the skills that industry needs. Advocates for higher education also need to work comfortably with government agencies responsible for policy setting and finance.

5.1.2.8. Supportive Legal and Regulatory Structure

Higher education institutions flourish in a legal and regulatory environment that encourages innovation and achievement, while discouraging corruption, duplication of effort and exploitation of poorly informed consumers. In many institutions, initiative is stifled by counterproductive legal constraints and centralised decision-making. Higher education is focused on people—regulation needs to foster, not hamper, human potential.

5.1.2.9. System-wide Resources

Many tools for improving higher education work best when developed centrally and shared widely. Such tools include management information systems, standardised tests, curriculum and 'knowledge banks' (repositories of information accessible through electronic means). They effectively and efficiently spread the financial and technical burdens of higher education development, allowing multiple institutions to work together.

No institution of higher education can hope to serve its students or the national interest, without developing a robust technological capacity. Higher education institutions need to encourage all constituent institutions, both public and private, to incorporate advances in computing and communications technology into their administrative structures, their teaching and their research. HAE can expand its reach to remote rural areas through distance education if it has access to appropriate technology and the capacity to use it effectively. In the 21st century this capability is an essential attribute of higher education.

5.1.3. Policy Directions and Issues

Higher education and HAE cannot be left to market forces in the hope that these will provide the type of education that serves the national and public interest. The government must ensure that the public interest is served and that basic research relevant to the country's needs is undertaken. Within the framework of state control governments own, finance, and operate higher education institutions.

Without careful monitoring this can lead to politicians appointing vice-chancellors and ministries dictating degree requirements and curricula. Instances of political pressure forcing HE and HAE institutions to increase student intake with the consequent dilution of education, facilities and morale are not uncommon. It is therefore necessary to create buffer mechanisms to provide a balance between state responsibility to protect and promote the public's interest with an individual institution's need for academic freedom and autonomy.

5.1.3.1. A Balance is Needed to Enable HAE to Function Effectively

To provide the balance, HE and HAE, need the support of formally constituted and credible entities that help make the case for education and its growth and delivery to the organs of government with the legal and fiscal power to ensure that adequate support is available and that the public and national interest is being served. Buffer mechanisms consist of statutory bodies that include representatives of the government, institutions of higher education, the private sector and other important stakeholders such as NGOs, farmer's organisations and student organisations. Among these may be found:

- Councils of higher education, including HAE to advise the government on the size, shape, and funding of higher education; often they are also responsible for quality assurance, promotion mechanisms and accreditation;
- Research councils or agencies that fund and promote research;
- Professional councils that focus on specific areas of higher education; and
- Governing councils (or boards of trustees) that guide and advise education institutions and policy-makers. These councils must be representative of all concerned stakeholders.

To be effective, these bodies require clear mandates, well-established operating procedures and full autonomy from both government and academia.

5.2. Major Challenge for HAE

Many have argued that HAE must change and, indeed, change pathways have been identified and some renamed and reoriented courses have emerged over the past decade or so but widespread and large-scale change examples remain elusive. The challenge now is for agricultural education to accept or ignore the opportunity to become part of a major shift in focus from production agriculture to rural development.

HAE is now in a third wave of change that impacts heavily on its role—the first being production agriculture, the second environment and now rural development. It could be argued that much of higher agricultural education missed the leadership opportunity offered by the second wave of change despite widespread support from a broad spectrum of rural and urban stakeholders and is still struggling to catch up. The focus on rural development offers another opportunity to HAE to claim and reclaim leadership in spearheading what promises to be a major international attempt to solve the problems associated with revitalising rural areas, poverty reduction and food security.

The widespread interest in rural development and poverty alleviation offers an opportunity that should be grasped. HAE can lead a process of defining the needs of the rural development and poverty alleviation process by:

- Inviting key stakeholders to engage in dialogue;
- Once needs are identified and agreed upon stakeholders can decide on their roles in supporting and guiding the process;
- The role and mission of HAE in supporting ERD should emerge from this exercise. HAE's detailed role will most likely show that internal organisational adjustments have to be made in HAE if it is to fulfil its role effectively;
- Armed with this analysis HAE is in a strong position to work on its own reform agenda. Here again the key reform element, leadership, emerges. Without the vision, the

belief, the energy, the ability to communicate effectively and the willingness to form partnerships, reforms will not take place.

5.2.1. Funding is Critical to the Reform

Reform of HAE entities and ensuring their involvement with education for rural development is not cost neutral. If, for example, the HAE entity is to support other education and training levels with teacher training, teaching materials and team teaching, funds to enable this to happen must be available. Without such an incentive little change will take place. Policymakers need to back all new or revised policies with the resources required to fully implement them. Income-generating activities could include executive training programmes, marketing the experience of faculty and offering services such as laboratory testing and rental of facilities.

5.2.2. Higher Agricultural Education Institutions

Once focused on the provision of agronomists for the farm economy, higher agricultural education (HAE) institutions are now facing new challenges, such as a decline of employment in agriculture, competition from other providers, expanding students' diversity and the digital divide between rural and urban areas. Over the years, innovative HAE institutions managed to reinvent themselves in order to meet the changing needs of rural areas and economies.

The most significant and eloquent change within HAE institutions is probably the redefinition of their missions. Hence, HAE institutions are evolving into multipurpose institutions geared towards meeting the local economy's needs in skills and knowledge. In many countries, serving and promoting the development of agriculture through agricultural education, research and extension have long been the three fundamental missions of HAE institutions.

The vision of HAE institutions, as reflected in the way they are redefining their missions, has deep repercussions on the nature and the content of their activities as well as on the resources, mechanisms and procedures they mobilise to implement their new mandate.

5.2.2.1. *Transformation and Diversification of HAE Institutions Activities*

Provision of Knowledge and Skills to Students

The forces shaping the transformation of HAE have changed the composition of the student body as well as the programmes offered and the learning process. China provides a clear illustration of this threat. Hence, HAE institutions' graduates are hardly willing to dedicate themselves to agricultural and rural development, although most of the students (about 60 per cent in the provincial agricultural universities) come from rural areas, including about one-third from poor areas. After graduation, most students prefer to look for a job in urban areas, even for positions not directly related to their field of study, rather than working in their remote and poor hometowns, although for decades the government has encouraged, including through incentives, graduates to return or to go to rural remote areas, the situation has not improved very much.

In many countries, besides depressed labour market prospects, the increasing competition of other higher education providers has contributed to make admission into HAE institutions problematic. Due to less competitive employment opportunities compared with other sectors, such as information technology, electronic industries and other high-tech sectors, HAE institutions are increasingly in competition with other universities to admit good candidates.

In China, the best students do not select HAE institutions as their first option after they pass the national enrolment examination. This affects the entire education quality of HAE. Agricultural universities do not efficiently conduct promotion campaigns. Both student candidates and their parents do not have sufficient information about agriculture and agricultural universities. In the meantime, integrated science and technology universities, MBA programmes and high-tech faculties enrol the best candidates. The competition for the local agricultural universities was the most unequal. That was a reason for merging them with provincial science and technology universities.

With some exceptions like China and Malawi, in many countries the drop in intake level and total enrolment became a major problem for HAE institutions. Reversing this trend and sustaining the attractiveness of their offerings have called for new strategies.

Academic Organisation and Curricula

Updating existing programmes, developing new ones and opening courses in different areas, are part of the usual response developed by higher education institutions to keep up with the expansion of knowledge, the rise of new technologies and the renewal of vocational skills and occupational structures. But the revision of curricula is also strongly correlated with the diversification of HAE institutions' missions. Besides technical knowledge and socio-economic relevance, the increasing recognition of core competencies contributes to curricula change in HAE institutions. Furthermore, the organisation of the curricula is affected by a trend towards modularisation and efforts to develop multidisciplinary approaches to teaching.

HAE institutions find it very easy to add new programmes to meet new needs. It is often tougher for them to adjust and to innovate by changing the focus of existing programmes. Reforms involving the elimination of obsolete programmes or the deep transformation of existing ones are even more painful and sometimes difficult to conceive. Most of the institutions studied here went through such processes.

The main change was to move from a mission-oriented formation to form professionals and graduates, with levels of excellence in their area of expertise, to a mission oriented one to form persons with a strong commitment for the development of their community. The graduated students are expected to make an impact upon the social, economic and political sectors and to be competitive in their area of expertise at the international level. In order to achieve this mission, the teaching/learning process and the extra-academic activities for the students must develop certain abilities, values and attitudes to foster this sense of commitment towards the community.

The students' abilities that needed to be reinforced include the capacity to (i) learn by themselves, (ii) the capacity of analysis, synthesis and evaluation, critical thinking and creativity, (iii) the capacity to identify and solve problems, (iv) the capacity to work in groups, (v) the efficient use of information technology, (vi) proficiency in English language and effective oral and written communication. The values and attitudes that the institution promotes include honesty, responsibility, leadership, entrepreneurship, innovation, and a spirit of constant improvement, among others.

In China the reform of HAE involved various measures to improve quality and relevance of delivery. Main changes include:

- Introducing flexibility through optional courses, representing 25 per cent to 30 per cent of total requested credits. After the students fulfil the compulsory courses, they can select relevant courses from other colleges or faculties to suit their own interests;
- Merging the relevant courses into block modules or seminars. The new curriculum for rural development was officially included in the national university faculty directory with the name of 'regional rural development'.
- Learning process. The development of work-experience programmes constitutes a major evolution in delivery systems. This increasing attention for developing such a capacity among graduates reflects the growing importance of lifelong learning to ensure that people stay up to date with fast changing market trends and technological change. Finally, HAE institutions are also increasingly relying on information and communication technologies (ICTs) to diversify oncampus modes of learning as well as to expand delivery to reach offcampus learners.

Working with and for the Rural Community

The ultimate success in improving the quality and relevance of HAE institutions depends to a large extent on the support of stakeholders. Traditionally, HAE institutions have trained students for employment, often in the public sector, not for self-employment. Yet, small business development seems a logical strategy for poor rural communities that are unlikely to attract external productive investment. Fostering new entrepreneurs therefore requires that the HAE institutions refocus their programmes. It is however important to differentiate self-employment and entrepreneurship and to recognise the complexity of the task.

Low-developed economies depend on self and family employment but display a poor record in entrepreneurship. In OECD countries, where waged employment is the reference, experience and business failure rates show that relatively few manage to be successful entrepreneurs.

Globalisation Strategies

People in rural areas are as much affected by globalisation as urban dwellers. Yet, they have fewer opportunities to benefit from it through establishing productive links with the rest of the world. Increasingly, HAE institutions, through their co-operation programmes, are developing such linkages.

The internationalisation strategy has also an impact upon staff training. Lectures and courses given by visiting professor are common. Recently, it was decided that at least two courses of the whole curricula must be taught in English. Thus, proficiency in the English language for students and staff is mandatory.

At the University of Cordoba, the international strategy offers the opportunity to exchange experiences with other countries at various levels: involvement of lecturers from European universities and institutions in the degree programme, opportunities for students to further their studies at other European and South American universities or to pursue Intensive Study Programmes or European Modules in conjunction with other European Universities under the Socrates-Erasmus European Community Programmes.

In 2001, the international character of the studies was further strengthened by significantly increasing teacher and student exchanges as well as international programmes. The affiliation of the Rural Development Research Group to various international university networks, together with the traditional willingness of the university to exchange teachers and students with other universities within Spain and elsewhere, is creating a very favourable atmosphere for the insertion, in international circles, of the studies and the students alike.

5.2.2.2. *Planning, Governance, Staff and Financing Issues*

Strategic Planning

Placed in a challenging context, HAE institutions use strategic planning methods to analyse economic opportunities and educational needs in the region, articulate vision and set development goals. Academic indicators support the constant improvement of the teaching/learning process. In general terms, the indicators evaluate aspects related to the performance of the staff, academic programmes and course content within the teaching/learning process. The students evaluate several aspects, including:

- evaluation of the subject for the course
- respect towards students by the teacher
- promotion of the self-learning process
- promotion of participation and research
- promotion of the appropriate use of the technology
- facilitate the learning of the subjects
- facilitate the development of abilities, values and attitudes
- assessment scheme.

The evaluation of these aspects is carried out each academic term using the electronic facilities of the school. The progress of the learning/ teaching process is monitored using this evaluation mechanism.

In China, the reform of HAE took place within a carefully designed planning approach involving the following steps:

- identification and diagnosis of the internal and external problems and constraints encountered during the national economic reform.
- formulation of the strategy, concept and guidelines of the HAE institutions' reform according to the identified problems and constraints and integration into the national institutional reform.
- launching in some universities of the pilot reform regarding internal structures and merging.
- implementation of the HAE institutions' reform in the whole country through multi-institutional co-operation and co-ordination.

Administrative Structure and Governance

Implementing diversified missions and activities requires appropriate administrative structures and governance mechanisms. Various aspects are at stake. One relates to decision-making processes and the nature and intensity of responsibility shared within the institution as well as with its constituency. Another aspect concerns the structure of the institution, taking into account its mandate as well as external expectations and constraints. Finally the sharing of authority between the various levels of management represents a key variable to understanding institutional change. While some examples relate directly to a particular issue, more complex processes affect administrative structure and governance through multiple ways like the reform in China.

In China, changing the internal administrative structure of HAE institutions constitutes an important element of the reform. Integration of the relevant functions of university departments or divisions has increased efficiency. Consequently, the number of administrative staff was reduced by 30-40 per cent. The redundant administrative staff was transferred to the logistic services and to student management departments. To further address the issue of efficiency, existing HAE institutions were merged with provincial universities. A large scale-merging plan was following a pilot phase. Four types of mergers were implemented:

- 'Strong-weak merging': Strong HAE institutions merged with the weak ones;
- 'Strong-strong merging': Several strong HAE institutions formed a new, stronger and larger institution with more faculties covering all professional areas needed by the labour market;
- 'Weak-weak merging': Integrating weak HAE institutions together for strengthening the capacities and more effective utilisation of relevant resources;
- Merging education institutions with research institutions: before the reform the co-operation between HAE institutions and research institutions was very weak; sometimes they competed for research fund allocation. Merging the HAE institutions and research institutions

provides more practice places for students and research institutions are able to use HAE institutions facilities for conducting their research activities.

The results and impacts of different types of merging are quite different. For 'strong-strong merging', efficiency and effectiveness have significantly improved. For 'strong-weak merging', in some cases former strong bodies discriminated against the weaker ones in terms of funds allocation and internal resource distribution.

For all types of merging, the overall internal administrative and coordination costs have increased. This was sometimes partly due to the fact that merged institutions were located in the different areas.

After the reform, most of the administration functions of local HAE institutions were decentralised and transferred to the provincial government or directly to institutions. Decentralised functions include the financial planning and investment budget, personnel development planning and recruitment, planning of enrolment and employment of students. HAE institutions can enlarge and diversify financial sources by mobilising other sources at the local level, including university-affiliated enterprises, but also from foreign investors. The increased amount of the education fees received from the students has improved the financial situation for HAE institutions with high reputations.

Under the policy guidance of the local government, HAE institutions can set up their institutional strategy and formulate development plans according to needs of provincial agricultural and rural development. The decentralisation also reduced the administrative layers. This change has significantly improved overall education efficiency. After the reform, governmental functions are mainly concentrated at the macro-level, institutional and policy guidance.

In the Ukraine, the Central Government plays an important role in the formulation and adaptation of programmes according to the needs of the economy. The Ministry of Education (MOE) is responsible for formulating the national higher education directory and supervising its implementation. The directory is normally updated every five years. During this period, universities can submit proposals and applications to the Curriculum and Degree Programme Administration of the Ministry of Education (MOE).

Staff Issues

The concept of the learning organisation is progressively penetrating the field of HAE. Increasingly it is felt that performance depends on learning. Given the accelerating pace of rural transformation, HAE institutions must absorb new knowledge, including beyond their traditional fields of interest and responsibility. Addressing this challenge requires HAE institutions to develop a staff development culture but also to adapt new forms of staff management, particularly for countries in transition.

In 1992 an official document indicated that "in order to achieve levels of excellence and high quality, ITESM adopted the philosophy of continuous improvement". As a result of this philosophy, each faculty member must be trained in teaching techniques for higher education. Staff are classified in three categories, (i) teaching staff, (ii) staff dedicated to consulting and (iii) staff dedicated to research. This categorisation illustrates the diversity of the missions of the institution.

Traditionally, a large part of the activity of the professor was dedicated to research. However, more recently, the proportion of time dedicated to develop and master teaching techniques, particularly with the introduction of information technology to the classroom, balanced out the time spent on teaching and research.

In China, before the reform, teaching and research staff in agricultural universities were employed as civil servants. Once a staff member was recruited the employment period was not limited, this meant, he/she could work up until official retirement age. HAE institutions had no right to terminate the employment relation even if the staff could not provide the expected services to their institutions. With the introduction of the socalled 'dynamic staff recruiting system' with an average contract period of two years, life-time employment is now over.

Another important area of reform concerns salary. Since 2000, most of the universities reformed the salary and payment mechanism by increasing the salary and income of teaching and research staff. In the new system, income will take into account some elements of performance-based salary. If the students' evaluation results and the overall annual work performance have not reached the minimum qualification pre-described for the position, they are transferred to a lower position with lower pay. It is expected that this system will create a pressure on staff members for improving their qualification and work performance according to the job descriptions advertised.

Financing

Finding resources to sustain institutions and implement change, is often difficult in low-income contexts. Resources come from students' fees but they also combine various other private sources including:

- student fees (approx. 50 per cent);
- financial support from the Board of Trustees (15 per cent);
- incomes from periodic Sorteos Tec (Raffles) (20 per cent);
- extension, continuous education and applied research (5 per cent);
- financing campaigns (aimed mostly at private enterprises) (10 per cent).

In China, the reform of HAE included various measures to renovate the financing of institutions. Within the new system sources of income include:

- Education funds allocated by the government to HAE institutions according to the number of students, making up about 31 per cent of the total income.
- Research funds received from governmental institutions and agricultural and agrochemical enterprises make up about 22 per cent of the total available budget, among which the government allocated research funds representing 90 per cent.
- Other funds allocated by the central and local governments for infrastructure improvement and financial support for daily operation constitute about 8 per cent, of which 79 per cent are from central government and 21 per cent from local government. Central government funds for HAE institutions' infrastructure improvements are mainly allocated to the national key universities, investment to the provincial and lower level institutions is very limited. The

infrastructure of HAE institutions in the Western provinces is still very poor, this being due to the limitation of government funds.

– Tuition fees from learners, income from the various income-generating education and training activities, such as on-campus short-term training courses, self-financed adult education, distance learning programmes and income transferred by the affiliated enterprises.

Through the students' enrolment reform, the resource gap, which has mostly depended on the governmental education fund, has been significantly reduced. The diversification strategy constitutes the most important improvement in HAE institutions' financial situation.

Criteria for Success

HAE institutions used to define their priorities from inside. Today they need to be responsive to external demands and take on new responsibilities to foster rural development. As a result HAE institutions tend to become more entrepreneurial, more sensitive to the needs of the rural learners, more dedicated to outreach activities and more community focused. Institutional leadership and the competence and commitment of key personnel play a large role in the success of any effort for change.

Institutional flexibility also constitutes an important criterion. Innovative institutions are open to new ideas and ready to build their capacity to take on their new roles. In addition to internal factors, institutional change can be hampered, or fostered, by the overall legal and policy frameworks in which an institution operates. Some institutions are very autonomous within their systems and can initiate programmes or take initiatives.

References

Acker, D. (Ed.), "Leadership for higher education in agriculture", *Proceedings of the inaugural conference of the Global Consortium of Higher Education and Research for Agriculture*, Ames, Iowa: Iowa State University, 1999.

Bawden, R., "Agricultural education and training: future perspectives", *Paper prepared for the Agricultural Knowledge and Information Systems (AKIS) thematic team in the Rural Family of the World Bank*, 1998.

Brown II, C. (Ed.), "Organization and governance in higher education (Fifth edition)", *ASHE Reader Series,* Boston: Pearson Custom Publishing, 2000.

Kunkel, H.O.; Maw, L.; Skaggs, C.L., (Eds), *Revolutionizing higher education in agriculture, framework for change,* Ames, IA: Iowa State University Press, 1996.

Liu, Y.; Jingzun, Z., "The reform of higher agricultural education institutions in China", *Case study prepared for IIEP,* 2002.

Melnychuk, D., *The reform of higher agricultural education institutions in Ukraine,* National Agricultural University of Ukraine, 2002.

Szekely, C., "Effects of structural and functional change in agriculture on the development of higher agricultural education in Europe", *Paper presented at the 4th European Conference on Higher agricultural education,* Moscow, 1998.

6

Educating Girls for Rural Development

Educating girls saves children's lives. The more time girls spend in school, the more likely they are to grow up to be mothers who are healthy, well-nourished, economically empowered and resourceful when it comes to the health and education of their children. These women have fewer children, healthier pregnancies and safer deliveries. Their babies are more likely to survive childbirth, the vulnerable first month of life and the critical first five years—laying the foundation for healthy and productive lives.

Educated girls marry later and have fewer children than uneducated girls. Studies in Africa, Asia and Latin America found that women with seven or more years of schooling married five years later than women with less or no education and had two to four fewer children. Educated women are also more likely to use contraception to delay or space their pregnancies at healthier intervals, which reduces the incidence of low birth weight babies, infant death and infant malnutrition.

A study in Zimbabwe found that "better educated women are much more likely to have ever used a modern contraceptive method than women without any schooling." And women who have completed primary education are 20 per cent more likely to use modern family planning than women who have no education, while women who have completed 12 or more years of schooling are nearly 50 per cent more likely.

Educated women tend to control a greater share of the household income, and this contributes to the well-being of all children. Mothers are more likely than fathers to invest their earnings in health care and in better quality food and education for both their girls and boys. One study found that the impact of income on child survival is 20 per cent higher if the money is brought in by the mother than by the father. Educating girls also helps prevent children from dying as a result of malnutrition or disease.

Another study found that children born to mothers who have been educated are half as likely to suffer from malnutrition or to die before the age of 5 as children born to mothers who did not complete primary school. Educated mothers are much more likely to immunise their children.

6.1. Education against AIDS

Because AIDS is a preventable disease with no known cure, basic education remains the strongest weapon against it. Girls who are educated have the knowledge and self-confidence to protect themselves against HIV and to prevent its transmission to the next generation. More girls than boys are HIV-positive in developing countries. In Africa, for every boy newly infected with HIV, there are between three and six girls newly infected. Where girls are not educated, HIV tends to spread more rapidly.

Simply keeping girls in school longer is an effective defence against HIV. Studies in Uganda and Zimbabwe found that girls who received primary and some secondary education had lower HIV infections rates than those who did not attend school, a trend that extended into early adulthood. For girls and women who are reluctant to talk openly about AIDS due to its social stigma, reading becomes a life-saving skill, offering a private way to learn about risk, protection and treatment.

Educated mothers, even if they are infected, are more likely to seek medical care during pregnancy and to use simple, inexpensive measures during labour and immediately after childbirth that can reduce the transmission of HIV from mother to child by more than 50 per cent. Some 39 million people worldwide are living with HIV or AIDS, 25 million of whom are in sub-Saharan Africa. The epidemic has left 15 million children orphaned.

Educated girls grow up to be literate women who are better prepared to make informed political choices. Education also gives them the self-confidence they need to engage in political discussion and to influence decisions. A study in Bangladesh found that educated women are three times as likely as illiterate women to participate in political meetings. And in Nepal, almost half of rural women who completed a nine-month literacy course said that they would be confident about expressing their views to the community, compared with only 4 per cent of non-literate women. When Uganda established mandatory quotas for representation of women on local councils, the allocation of funding for health facilities improved. When Liberian women organised themselves to press for a "women's initiative," they successfully advocated for a new unit for women and children in the Ministry of Planning and convinced the Ministry of Education to start a mass literacy drive aimed at girls. And when women in Guatemala joined forces, they successfully pushed for better policies guaranteeing health care, education and economic opportunities to women and children.

In emergency situations—such as earthquakes, floods and armed conflict—education for girls plays an especially important role in protecting against some of the worst forms of harm and abuse. Conflicts and natural disasters destabilise social infrastructure, leaving all children, and especially girls, vulnerable to threats such as sexual violence, exploitative labour and trafficking. The lack of access to education and basic services, as well as the emotional trauma of disasters, takes an enormous toll on all children.

Girls dropping out of school is often one of the first indicators of stress or instability in a community. As families struggle to survive, girls are pulled from school to support the family. Insecurity can also reduce access to education, as schools may become targets for recruitment and abduction, or girls may be attacked along the path to school. Due to worries of security, the proportion of girls not attending school during a period of conflict tends to be much higher than the proportion of boys out of school. Moreover, rape is an increasingly common weapon of war in many parts of the world. A high proportion of girls become mothers at a dangerously early age, and these girls often cannot attend school because of lack of child care, community stigma and the belief that once a girl has children she is an adult and therefore beyond the age of needing education.

Formal and informal educational opportunities for girls caught in crisis situations help both to prevent some of these tragic consequences and to heal those who have suffered. Preschools and schools can be safe places where girls and boys are out of harm's way and accounted for. Classes provide a sense of normalcy, routine and hope for the future that is critical to emotional well-being. Well-designed educational programmes also introduce new survival skills—for example, children may be taught how to avoid land mines, protect themselves against sexual abuse, deal with anger or resolve interpersonal conflicts.

Keeping girls in school helps set the stage for quicker recovery once a crisis has passed. And by equipping the next generation of mothers with the knowledge and skills to raise healthy, well-educated children, it can help prevent the recurrence of violence and chaos. There is also evidence that educated women play a vital role in helping to save lives and rebuild communities after natural disaster has struck. Where girls are educated, mothers are more likely to take the complex health measures required to protect their families' well-being. Monetary savings levels are likely to be higher, which gives families more resources to recover. And communities where women are educated are also more likely to have civil society groups to help the most vulnerable reclaim their lives.

6.2. Girls' Education and Boarding Schools

Boarding schools, referred to as residential schools or feeder hostels, are educational institutions with dormitory facilities where students may live or board during the school year. The dormitories have sleeping, lavatory, eating, study and recreational areas. There is often accommodation for teaching and support staff. Schools can be integrated or segregated. They can be for a particular ethnic or minority group, open to students in a specified area, or for those with unique qualifications and characteristics. Dormitory facilities may be separated by sex, age, or even familial relationship when families send more than one child. Dormitories most often are located on the school campus.

Children of remote and rural—usually minority -populations in Nepal, China and Viet Nam, as well as nomadic children in Mongolia and Central Asia, have benefited from education in boarding schools. Some boarding schools, such as those for the Khmer in Viet Nam, have been initiated by leaders of ethnic minorities in order to enhance their children's educational foundation through schools that both strengthen ties with the majority culture and maintain their own. Some countries in Central Asia, during their socialist years, were able to achieve near universal basic education due, in part, to boarding schools. Remote rural populations in those countries not only accept, but expect, boarding facilities to support basic education.

Many African countries have a long boarding school tradition, particularly at the secondary level. This practice dates back to the colonial period. Today, there are still boarding schools in parts of Englishspeaking Africa that are modelled on the British experience. Indeed, in many ways, little has changed since those days: The distance from village communities to secondary schools continues to make secondary education inaccessible to many children. As a result, many children drop out of school after the primary level. In this context, boarding schools play a key role in providing secondary education. Furthermore, in a number of African countries, student meals are government subsidised so that it may cost less for parents to have their children fed a comparable diet in boarding schools than at home.

In Ghana, boarding schools comprise some 80 per cent of all schools. In fact, some parents believe that schools do a better job of bringing up children than they can. However, in recent years, there has been a tendency in Africa to discontinue boarding schools due to governmental fiscal "belttightening."

6.2.1. Advantages

When managed and operated properly, boarding schools can yield benefits for students, parents and educators. Some of these are discussed below:

Promote access to schooling: The primary goal of state boarding schools is to increase access to learning opportunities of children from underserved and disadvantaged communities. Boarding facilities, for example, make schooling for many rural children possible.

Attain gender equality in enrolment, retention and achievement. A study in Nepal showed that feeder hostels for girls promoted girls' enrolment, retention and achievement in education. Feeder hostels bring girls from remote and rural areas of the country, where opportunity for obtaining secondary education does not exist. These hostels provide food and accommodation and, most importantly, an opportunity to attend a secondary school. Upon completion of their schooling, the girls are encouraged to take up teaching, thereby becoming important role models for the girls who follow. Tamil Nadu in India and the Central Highland provinces of Viet Nam are advocating more hostel facilities for girls to increase enrolment and retention in secondary school.

In some cultures, parents are reluctant to send their children, especially girls, to school. In many countries, parents of poor and large families require children's labour for food production and for care of younger siblings. Despite state subsidies, there are generally costs attached to sending children to school that parents often cannot meet. In such cases, boarding schools may provide a reasonable transitional arrangement.

Provide improved learning environments to children. Boarding schools can be a choice for many families that cannot offer adequate facilities for study. Where homes are overcrowded and do not have electricity, boarding schools can offer a better study environment.

Enhance academic performance of children, especially girls. Boarding schools are believed to help enhance academic performance of children. Boarding schools enhance girls' academic performance since they do not have to spend time going long distances to schools and are not burdened by domestic chores at home. Boarding schools in eastern and southern Africa are generally same-sex schools, and it has been shown that academic performance among girls is higher than in co-educational schools.

Give security and protection to girls. In societies where girls' movement outside home is not permitted, boarding schools can give security and protection. In Mongolia, for instance, rural parents are more likely to encourage girls than boys to continue schooling because they perceive that boarding schools offer personal protection and education that ensures their daughters of future jobs; conversely, boys are perceived to be better able to fend for themselves.

Protect children in emergency situations. Boarding schools have been an important protection for children at risk of emergencies, such as from natural disasters or civil wars. At times, schools can continue their operations. Students from flood-, winter disaster- and other calamity-prone areas have been ensured shelter, food, education and recreation during the disaster. In Nepal, non-governmental organisations (NGOs) are operating hostels to offer shelter and education to street children and those displaced by ongoing conflict.

Meet nutritional needs of children. Experience from Mongolia and Viet Nam shows that well-managed boarding schools provide good nutrition, hygiene, and sanitation; a balanced daily routine of personal care; education; assistance for the boarding school community; sports and recreation; and study habits that children introduce to their own homes and families and to their lives as adults.

Promote socialisation and mainstreaming of poor and minority children. Boarding schools can be a means of socialising and mainstreaming children coming from rural and remote areas and those belonging to ethnic and linguistic minorities. Children are introduced to new ways of living; new routines and responsibilities; new technologies; and new teachers and fellow students from outside their community.

Provide effective links between the community and the larger society. Boarding schools provide a centralised location for learning and living that can be an effective link between the remote communities of origin and the larger society. Children from remote communities increase their options for the future by learning skills that will assist them in contributing to their own communities, in adapting to the larger community, or in bridging the two.

Reduce the cost of educating children. Where settlements are highly scattered and populations are sparse, it can be extremely costly to establish and operate full-fledged schools. Studies in Nepal have shown that it is very costly to run schools in the high mountains, where the average number of students per school is less than 25. Small schools are generally not cost effective in a centralised bureaucracy. Boarding or residential schools can, therefore, be established where it is not feasible to establish and operate a small community school. The Government of Nepal is considering establishing residential schools in the mountain districts by merging very small schools. Analysis shows that providing education through boarding schools would be much cheaper than the existing system, where education is provided through very small schools scattered throughout the districts.

6.2.2. Disadvantages

Boarding schools are not without problems and disadvantages.

Boarding schools contribute to cultural extinction: Boarding schools are viewed as a threat to the child's culture. In the last part of the 19th and the first half of the 20th Centuries in North America and Australia, boarding schools were a key aspect of policies focused at assimilating indigenous children into a dominant European-oriented society through language, lifestyle, education and religion. Compulsory education enforced a culture and curriculum alien to the indigenous population. Boarding schools played a major role in the extinction of indigenous native cultures, languages and religions.

Boarding schools cause cultural illiteracy. Some believe that children attending boarding schools can become culturally illiterate. Being away from home at an early age means being unable to learn many cultural values, beliefs, practices, and customs that are needed to function effectively in the community. Once these children return to their communities, a profound loss of identity may result.

Boarding schools cause a sense of alienation. Boarding schools are physically and emotionally isolating from families and communities. Children staying in boarding schools can develop feelings of not being loved, wanted or cared for. It can have negative effects on children's learning achievement and growth.

Boarding schools may increase the risk of physical and sexual abuse. Some studies have reported that children are at higher risk of abuse in boarding schools. Such incidents of physical and sexual abuse may never get reported, and children live with the pain of abuse throughout their lifetimes.

Girls are at risk of pregnancy and dropping out. Zimbabwean and Nigerian research indicates that girls in boarding schools are at risk of becoming pregnant and then dropping out of schools. The risk of pregnancy prevents parents from sending adolescent girls to boarding schools.

Children's growth and learning may be harmed. Where sufficient state and/or local budgets are not available to meet the costs of running boarding schools, the health of children is at risk. Under-funded boarding schools that are not maintained and repaired can compromise health as children suffer from cold, dampness or coal smoke fumes; insufficient or inadequate food; poor attendance of teachers; and low quality teaching/a poor social environment that leads to a poor education. Eventually parents lose their confidence in the school system. If boarding schools are not properly staffed and resourced, they can ruin the health, as well as the schooling, of children.

Girls may be discriminated against. Where dormitories are unsupervised and under-funded, such as those built by communities and not attached to the school, girls can be overly burdened by domestic chores. Where girls have to find their own accommodation, they risk becoming housemaids to male students or host families. In these situations, the girls' education is compromised.

6.3. Strategies for Girls' Education

The strategies that follow, whether working from inside or outside the classroom, have been proven to increase school attendance and completion by girls. Each promotes in its own way the model of a school that seeks to ensure effective learning in safe, healthy gendersensitive and child-centred environments. No country could implement all of these strategies at once. Governments should undertake an analysis of the particular barriers facing girls as a necessary prelude to selecting a package of the most pertinent interventions. An opinion poll of the perceptions of parents and children of those barriers would play an important part in such an analysis.

Making education free and compulsory is the keystone of any national plan to eliminate gender disparity in education and achieve universal education. Faced with an economically driven choice between sending sons or daughters to school, poor families often send their sons. Removing fees or offering financial support to families with daughters in school, as well as explaining the advantages of sending girls to school, can make a real difference.

6.3.1. Strategies within the classroom

6.3.1.1. Child-centred and gender-sensitive classroom

Making the classroom more child-centred and gender-sensitive, and rooted in the life and environment of the community. Fore example, the Nueva Escuela Unitaria Bilingüe intercultural programme in Guatemala is founded on participatory teaching and learning, with play and study creatively combined. Teachers make full use of Mayan languages and culture that have in the past been marginalised despite their importance to half the country's population. The result is a completion rate above the national average and a high enrolment rate for girls.

6.3.1.2. Recruiting good teachers

Recruiting and training teachers who are sensitive to gender and child rights, and paying them a regular, living wage. Both female and male teachers should receive training in gender awareness in the classroom. Without this, some countries, such as Zambia, found that teachers may value and encourage boys' participation in class more than they value girls' and may allocate school tasks along strict gender lines, leaving girls to sweep the floors or clean the toilets. While one cannot assume that all women teachers are gender-sensitive in their teaching methods, there is a specific need in some areas to recruit more women teachers who can serve as role models for girls and may make girls' parents feel more comfortable. Countries that achieve higher enrolment in primary education tend to employ a high proportion of female teachers.

6.3.1.3. Promoting health in schools

In Myanmar, one programme adopts a holistic, life skills approach to health. The School-Based Healthy Living and HIV/AIDS Prevention Education programme is taught as part of the standard curriculum to children from grades 2 to 9. It focuses on a range of health and social issues—from HIV/AIDS to personal hygiene, from nutrition to drugs—and explores them through activities designed to develop life skills such as communication, cooperation and problem-solving.

6.3.1.4. Promoting sports in schools

Providing girls with access to sport can also contribute to achieving gender parity in education. With sports in many countries a traditionally male domain, girls' participation challenges gender stereotypes, breaking down entrenched attitudes. As female athletes gain recognition, they become mentors to others.

Through sports, girls are given the chance to be leaders and improve their confidence and self-esteem. As girls participate in sports, they acquire new interpersonal skills and through additional social networks gain access to different opportunities, allowing them to become more engaged in school and community life. In Romania, sport has increased school participation among the minority Roma community by providing an opportunity for girls and boys to participate in teams, conditional to school attendance and academic performance. In Zimbabwe, the Youth Education through Sport programme, led by young people, requires participants to commit themselves to staying in school and to volunteering in their communities. The programme's aim is for them to adopt life skills, become peer educators and contribute to their communities as positive role models.

6.3.1.5. Eliminating gender bias

Eliminating gender bias from textbooks and learning materials. Apart from the obvious value to girls, the thoughtful revision of textbooks, classroom materials and lesson plans is likely to increase their quality and relevance to the lives of all children. In Viet Nam, the Government is developing new gendersensitive teacher-training modules, ensuring that future textbooks are gender neutral, and providing training in gender and child rights to national education managers and members of local parent-teacher associations. In Somalia, a gender-based approach to curricula development and teacher training has increased enrolment by 28 per cent to more than 260,000. There is now a higher demand for education by parents and communities, and increased numbers of women are becoming active members of community education committees.

6.3.1.6. Scheduling lessons flexibly

Children are often excluded from school because of family responsibilities or the homework that is more often allocated to girls than boys. BRAC schools in Bangladesh have given priority to girls and inspired many other countries to follow their example. The school schedule is flexible; though it runs for two hours a day, six days a week, the times are set by local parents, and the school calendar is adapted to fit local considerations such as the harvest. BRAC schools met with such success that the scheme expanded quickly, and total enrolment is now at about 1.2 million. As a result of the programme's special emphasis on girls' enrolment, about 70 per cent of children in non-formal primary education and schools providing basic education for older children are female. Around 97 per cent of the teachers in BRAC schools are women.

6.3.1.7. Teaching in the local language

When the language of instruction is different from the children's mother tongue, it is often more disabling for girls, who tend to be less exposed to social environments beyond their immediate families. In Peru, girls and boys are first taught in Quechua, their mother tongue, and subsequently learn Spanish as a second language. The proposal for Intercultural Bilingual Education to be applied to multigrade classrooms and one teacher schools for native Quechua speakers in poor rural Andean areas has contributed to a 50 per cent increase in writing and communication abilities for girls and boys.

6.3.2. Strategies Outside the Classroom

6.3.2.1. Gathering gender-specific education statistics

Gathering gender-specific education statistics, including those on learning achievement at primary, secondary and tertiary levels.

6.3.2.2. Providing early childhood programmes

All children are likely to benefit from pre-school care, but evidence suggests that it enhances girls' preparedness for school more than boys'. What is more, it is the first point, after the family, at which gender stereotypes can be addressed.

6.3.2.3. *Enabling young mothers to return to school*

In many countries girls who become pregnant while at school are forbidden to return to their studies. The Forum for African Women Educationalists has been particularly active in lobbying governments in sub-Saharan Africa to change this policy. In Zambia, a 1997 policy allows re-admitting schoolgirls after they give birth, yet very few girls return due to perceived stigma and bullying from their peers. In Chile, the Ministry of Education in 1990 instructed schools not to expel any pregnant girl. However, the ruling proved difficult to enforce, and the Government submitted to Parliament a law, approved in 2000, guaranteeing the right of girls to continue and complete their education, while demanding from schools the necessary academic facilities.

6.3.2.4. *Taking special measures to reach the most disadvantaged girls.*

In some countries and regions where ethnic minorities, people living in rural areas and the poor face discrimination and exclusion, girls often suffer a multiple disadvantage because of their gender. The more disadvantaged the girl, the more essential it is that the education system should reach out to her through special measures, rather than just assuming she will be drawn in as part of a general drive for education for all. In Bhutan, 80 per cent of the population live by subsistence farming, scattered over mountain slopes rather than clustered in towns.

6.3.2.5. *Providing alternative education for girls*

One way of reaching girls who have dropped out of school, as well as other groups such as working children and children in conflict situations, is through education centres established outside the formal school system. In Turkey, learning centres in five provinces encourage girls normally confined to the home and domestic labour, to enrol in 'open primary school'. The centres perform an invaluable social as well as educational function; girls have organised field trips to neighbouring provinces and even drama clubs involving local boys. The Turkish Ministry of Education has adopted the open primary school as a model for its own girls' education strategy.

6.3.2.6. Providing alternative education for overaged children

In the United Republic of Tanzania, the Complementary Basic Education in Tanzania programme serves an estimated 3 million over age children and adolescents who are out of school. It provides basic education through a specially designed three year course, at the end of which children are eligible to join the mainstream school system. Girls were the initial focus of the project due to their low enrolment rates. But the difficulty in locating them, either because they were working indoors or they married, failed to adequately address gender in the enrolment process. It has been successful in reaching excluded or 'hidden' groups of children, including orphans, children of single parents and young mothers. The project has been mainstreamed into the formal education system to cater to all over age children and adolescents who will not be eligible to enter the school system under new rules that stipulate age as a condition for entry.

6.3.2.7. Locating schools closer to children's homes

Locating schools closer to children's homes, if necessary by establishing small, multigrade or multiage schools in remote rural areas. Girls are less likely to be able to make a long journey from home to school, not least because of concerns about their safety en route. Burkina Faso, for example, has developed a network of 'satellite schools'. These are small schools that accommodate only the first three grades, allowing the youngest children (who start school at the age of 7) to gain their first experience of school in or close to their own villages.

6.3.2.8. Making sure girls and boys are safe

This involves making schools secure not only from without—perimeter walls have, for example, been found to increase girls' sense of safety in many countries—but also from within. Education is a key to protection when it is of good quality, but falls short when the learning environment itself fails to provide the necessary protection against violence and abuse of children. When schools are associated with sexual or physical gender violence, girls' access to education is negatively affected. Parents will naturally hesitate to send their daughters to schools that are thought to be sites of physical or sexual gender violence. Boys and girls are often susceptible to psychological and physical violence in different ways, and adolescents in particular can find themselves especially vulnerable to violations of their safety.

6.3.2.9. *Encouraging girls' participation and activism for education*

Girls can be the most effective and inspiring advocates of child-friendly education if they are given the chance. The Girls' Education Movement is a dynamic pan-African girls' organisation supported by the Forum for African Woman Educationalists as well as by the Governments of Norway and Uganda. Launched in 2001, the Movement aims not just to galvanise action for education for all, but also to change the character of school systems so that "they offer rich, rewarding and friendly learning experiences for all children." Through the process of school mapping and the use of indigenous knowledge, the clubs were able to identify homes with out-of-school children, develop a list of all the children who were not going to school within the school's catchment area and take the initiative in bringing them to school. As a result, not only has girls' enrolment increased, but there has also been a shift in the way girls are perceived, from passive victims to active, vocal and engaged participants.

6.3.2.10. *Involving the local community*

The Community Empowerment Project in Jordan led to the village of Al-Rashedieh holding a community meeting, where women discussed their worries about their daughters being forced to stop school due to the absence of a secondary school for girls in the area. The women prepared a petition and went to plead their case with the director of the education ministry in Aqaba. Within six months, three fully equipped girls' secondary classes had been established. The Opening Doors for Girls' Education project in the rural Andean areas of Peru, which have been affected by extreme poverty and conflicts over the past two decades, involves 324,000 inhabitants of 540 communities in monitoring girls' inclusion in society and their right to a good education. This participatory monitoring strategy has benefited more than 65,000 girls. In Sudan, the Child-Friendly Community Project shows how community involvement made a difference in the number of girls in school and the quality of education for girls and boys alike.

6.3.2.11. Supplying safe water and latrines

Many girls drop out of school at the onset of menstruation, partly because there are no separate toilet facilities. Sometimes it is not enough simply to provide the latrines, however. Girls' involvement in identifying their location and type can be critical in determining whether they will be used. UNICEF has helped provide 1,400 schools in Pakistan with water and sanitation and is currently promoting school sanitation and hygiene in 46 other countries.

6.3.2.12. Decreasing the domestic workload

Many girls are kept at home to help with domestic tasks. Supplying communities or women's groups with equipment such as mills to grind cereals, huskers, carts and plastic barrels for water conservation, can decrease the amount of work to be done so that girls can be freed to attend school. Girls may also be prevented from going to school because they have to fetch water from a traditional well or remote water pump. Creating water points can alleviate their workload, as well as provide safe water for the whole community. Day-care community centres for children under six can relieve girls from looking after their siblings, thereby allowing them to go to school.

6.3.2.13. Making sure men and boys are involved

The rights and well-being of children are best served when relations between men and women in the household are based on mutual respect, equal rights and shared responsibilities. Men often can play unique and positive roles in the lives of children and often actively support efforts to reduce gender inequality.

6.4. Role of UNICEF

UNICEF believes that poverty reduction begins with children and that investments in children offer the best guarantee for achieving equitable and sustainable human development. As a tool for empowerment and sustainable development, education in particular can serve as a door to poverty reduction, with girls' education a key to unlocking its full transformative potential. This has been recognised in the MDGs for education and gender which take up the EFA goals of eliminating gender disparity in primary and secondary education by 2005 and in all levels of education no later than 2015, as well as ensuring that, by 2015, all children everywhere will be able to complete primary school. These targets are echoed in the World Fit For Children adopted at the Special Session for Children and are enshrined in the Convention on the Rights of the Child which recognises the right of all children everywhere to a quality education. It is widely recognised that without success on the education goals, prospects for achievement of the other international goals are dim.

UNICEF's focus on girls' education as an organisational priority is a strategic response to the call for quality basic education for all (EFA), enabling it to pursue its commitment to the MDG gender and education targets, the goals of the World Fit for Children, and the rights enshrined in the Convention on the Rights of the Child. UNICEF plays a leading role in advocating for girls' education to be viewed as an entry point to education for all children; as an issue that involves integrated action across sectors; as a matter of fulfilling the basic rights of all children to education; and as an approach that leverages progress for multiple goals both within and outside of the education sector. UNICEF believes strongly that girls' education is a key to breaking the intergenerational transmission of poverty and catalysing progress towards a host of positive development outcomes.

While progress has been made in providing quality basic education for an ever-increasing number of girls and in reducing the gender gap, it is clear that the world is not on track to achieving the 2015 goals and that the gender parity goal set for 2005 is rapidly slipping out of reach for some countries. Girls still make up the majority of the 115 million children out of school, with sub-Saharan Africa and South Asia particularly affected. As lead agency within the UN Girls' Education Initiative (UNGEI), UNICEF works with partners at many levels to accelerate action, shape strategies, and build the alliances that are so critical to achieving the goals.

In view of the urgency of the situation, UNICEF has developed a strategy for accelerating progress on girls' education in all countries, but with a special focus on intensive efforts in the 25 countries most at risk of failing to achieve the 2005 gender parity goals—20 of them in Africa and South Asia. This new strategy is designed to ensure maximum synergy with the Education-for-All Fast Track Initiative (FTI) spearheaded by the World Bank and other in initiatives in education.

At country level, UNICEF's programmes of support emphasise multi-sectoral strategies to expand access to education, to enhance educational quality, and to ensure positive learning achievements, with interventions designed to address some of the most persistent barriers to girls' education and to eliminate gender disparities. As gender disparities are often linked to other sources of inequality, holistic approaches are necessary to ensure equitable outcomes. For rural girls in particular, gender often intertwines with geography, poverty, ethnicity, and a host of other socio-cultural and economic factors to intensify the disadvantage in education.

The following examples illustrate some of the ways UNICEF is helping to address these issues and enhance progress towards the gender and education goals in rural areas.

6.4.1. Community Schools in Egypt

Since 1992, UNICEF has supported the Community Schools Initiative in Egypt, working in partnership with the Ministry of Education, NGOs and communities. The aim is to provide quality education for children living in small, rural hamlets in Upper Egypt where primary schools were previously non-existent and rural girls were particularly deprived (net enrolment rates for rural girls range from 50%-70%, compared with 90% nationally). Currently, the 200 community schools established by the project have reached some 6,000 children—70% girls. Modelled after the BRAC experience in Bangladesh, the schools are located in the communities themselves, and hidden costs—from uniforms to school bags—are removed.

Local ownership is a key feature of the project, with communities donating space, ensuring that children come to class, and managing the schools through a local education committee established in each hamlet. Young women with intermediate degrees are recruited locally and trained as facilitators to provide quality education through interactive techniques and the content of education is made relevant to local needs and interests, including health, environment, agriculture, and local history.

Graduates from community schools are eligible for exams in government schools at the end of grades 3 and 6.

The project is serving as a catalyst for development and change in gender roles and expectations for the girl students as well as the women facilitators. In a sign of national ownership, the Government has also developed a one room school initiative modelled in part on the principles of the community schools. UNICEF is now working closely with the Ministry of Education to expand the community school experience to areas where girls' enrolment is low and to streamline the quality components of the project into the mainstream education system, while strengthening national capacity for implementation of the model.

6.4.2. Education for Nomadic Children in Sudan

Nomadic populations the world over are often among the most impoverished of rural dwellers, their nomadic lifestyle itself seen as a major obstacle to the provision of basic services. In Sudan, where pastoral nomads make up about 8% of the population, nomadic children have been largely excluded from education. In the mid 1990s, fewer than 5% of nomadic boys and virtually no girls were attending primary school (compared to average national total gross enrolment of about 50%). The Education for Children of Nomads project was initiated in 1993 in Darfur states, where enrolment of children from nomadic communities was negligible. Based on a partnership between communities, state education authorities and UNICEF, the project supported the establishment of multi-grade, single -teacher schools for nomadic children that provided community-based education up to grade 4.

Now a decade old, the activities designed to increase learning opportunities for nomadic children have made substantial progress. The schools are accessible, because they move with the nomadic tribes. They are affordable, because costs are shared between government and the communities. They are appealing, because incentives offered by the community and the government attract good teachers who use good quality teaching materials provided by UNICEF. They are culturally appropriate, because they provide an educational environment that communities consider safe for their daughters.

By 2002, the nomadic education project had reached national dimensions, with more than 45,639 children enrolled in 651 UNICEF-supported nomad schools in 9 states, and demand continues to expand. Now, communities with schools are sometimes making migration choices based not only on the needs of their animals for grazing and water, but also on the needs of their children for education. "We now only move twice a year instead of 4 times", said one community leader, "because it is less disruptive to the school". A key challenge for the future lies in developing appropriate means of extending educational opportunities beyond grade 4.

6.4.3. Reaching Rural Girls in Yemen

Girls' education is a key challenge in Yemen, especially in rural areas where only 30% of school-age girls are enrolled. UNICEF's support has been designed to address basic obstacles to rural girls' participation in education, including lack of schools and lack of female teachers (women make up 20% of the teaching force overall, but only 8% of rural teachers). Activities aim to expand access through construction and rehabilitation of community schools built close to home; to improve quality through pre-service and in-service training of female teachers; and to strengthen awareness of the importance of education through information campaigns conducted through the media and through inter-personal communications by religious leaders.

Parent-teacher associations and communities are involved in school construction, which includes provision of separate toilets for girls to encourage attendance as well as provision of classroom furniture and equipment. Assessment has shown positive results in expanding access, with project activities undertaken in 17 districts in 5 governorates; as well as in stimulating more active participation of students in the learning process. But continuing challenges remain and will be addressed through support by UNICEF and other partners for the recently developed a National Strategy for Basic Education. Yemen is also part of the World-Bank led Fast Track Initiative.

6.4.4. Rural Indigenous Girls in Latin America

In Latin America, where overall enrolments are high, equity issues remain as a key concern, particularly for rural and indigenous populations who are often excluded from education. In Guatemala, for example, while 60% of the school-age population lives in rural areas, only 24.5% of the schools are found there: and while 50/100 urban students finish primary school, this drops to 20/100 for rural students (21 for rural boys; 17 for rural girls; 12 for indigenous children). Within the context of national education reform, UNICEF supports extended coverage of bilingual and inter-cultural schooling along with strengthened teacher training. In Bolivia, where net primary enrolment at national level has reached 93%, it is estimated that some 85,000 children aged 6-15 are still out of school—mostly in rural and indigenous areas where poverty is also concentrated. Difficulties in access and retention for rural, indigenous girls are particularly acute. UNICEF supports government efforts to extend bilingual, intercultural education, including through extensive social mobilisation and information campaigns and—through the Amazon sub-regional programme—training for indigenous teachers.

In Colombia, through the PROANDES sub-regional programme, UNICEF since 1999 has been promoting the child-friendly school initiative in departments characterised by the highest concentrations of indigenous populations and lowest indicators of education achievement. In many instances, a significant improvement was made on the overall quality of education based on the application of participatory methods in the learning process combined with improvements in overall school environment, including strengthened dialogue and relationships among children, teachers, parents and community.

In Peru, a UNICEF-supported programme of 'Opening Doors to Rural Girls' Education' has aimed since 1999 at promoting the right to education as well as the right to wider participation in society of indigenous girls living in rural areas. Parents, teachers, and other community members participate in community education committees which help to maintain a clean and healthy school environment, organise adult literacy classes, and identify out-ofschool children. These committees also develop educational materials and help raise awareness of children's right to an education and gender quality. Teachers report that the project has helped to change the attitudes of many community members, addressing the hidden, gender-based factors that contribute to girls' exclusion from quality education.

6.4.5. Ensuring the Rights of Rural Working Girls in Iran

Many children who are out of school around the world are engaged in child labour, constrained by poverty to work to support themselves and their families, often under hazardous conditions that represent an infringement of their basic human rights. As part of the disparity reduction programme in education in Iran, UNICEF supports education for rural working girls who have dropped out of school in disadvantaged provinces. The aims are to increase enrolment and completion rates; to train female teachers in new teaching and learning activities; and to promote life skills competency, vocational skills, and coping capacities. The project covers some 10,000 girls in 9 provinces, with positive outcomes in learning achievements and retention rates. It has also resulted in higher self esteem, communication skills and peer-bonding among the girls who participate. Through the project, the national literacy movement organisation has designed a new training curriculum for its teachers and has adapted educational material, assignments and classroom activities to suit the basic needs of rural girls. Future plans include a comprehensive intersectoral approach to advocacy and communication for quality girls' education.

6.4.6. IDEAL approach in Bangladesh

In Bangladesh, UNICEF supports the Intensive District Approach to Education for All (IDEAL), which promotes child-friendly, gender-sensitive schools covering over half of the 64 districts of the country. Among other things, the programme focuses on improving quality through support for multiple ways of teaching and learning and greater community involvement. Some 150,000 primary school teachers and supervisory staff have been trained in child-centred classroom techniques to make learning more child-centred and joyful, and tools for better monitoring of learning achievements are being developed.

Local-level planning has been strengthened and school management committees activated, with schools preparing annual school plans and catchment area maps through IDEAL interventions. By 2002, the IDEAL project had been expanded to cover 9.3 million children with 144,306 teachers in 36,109 schools, with assessment showing positive results in enhancing attendance, completion and learning achievement.

Social mobilisation is a key feature in national efforts to boost education for girls, with gender equity issues promoted and popularised through an innovative animated cartoon series known as MEENA, whose heroine serves as a role model to millions of girls. 'Meena Day' is observed nation-wide, with awareness raised through seminars, art competitions, group paintings by children, and story writing by children and teachers. Bangladesh is also well known for the extensive activities of the Bangladesh Rural Advancement Committee (BRAC), which has developed some of most effective and emulated strategies to address educational needs in poor rural communities.

6.4.7. Girls' Higher Quality Education in Balochistan (Pakistan)

In the remote rural areas of Balochistan province in southwestern Pakistan UNICEF has been assisting the government to boost enrolments of girls in primary schools and ensure quality teaching and learning. Balochistan is characterised by some of the lowest educational indicators in the country, particularly for girls. With the total participation rate in primary education estimated at 61% in 2002, girls' participation remained at a low of 23%. Educational opportunities for girls in rural areas are especially limited, as both facilities and female teachers are lacking and prevailing social customs often restrict girls and women to the home. Targeting communities in 4 districts where more than 35-40 girls aged 5-7 were not enrolled, the project has, since 1999, registered nearly 27,000 new enrolments, with a near 90% retention rate. This has been made possible through a community-wide promotion of girls' primary schooling involving community education committees and councils, community leaders, teachers and parents working together to create better opportunities for girls. In areas were there were no schools, 80 community supported process schools were established and teachers for them were recruited from the community and trained. The project is now working to consolidate and build upon gains to further increase access and to improve the quality of education through application of the child-friendly school concept in a total of 730 schools in the 4 districts.

6.4.8. Back to School in Afghanistan

After 23 years of conflict and a ban on girls' education under the Taliban, the back-to-school campaign supported by UNICEF in Afghanistan enabled 2.9 million children to return to school in 2002 (7,000 schools staffed by about 75,000 teachers). Girls' participation rose from 5% of total enrolments in 2001 to 30% in 2002. As part of the campaign, some 74,000 educational kits were assembled in neighbouring countries and teachers' orientation sessions were held on the new materials. Efforts were made to reach every known school with the needed educational supplies, including through mobilisation of 3,000 donkeys to gain access to remote rural areas. A far-reaching advocacy and community mobilisation campaign was organised with the Ministry of Education to encourage Afghan parents to send their children back to school.

Nation-wide monitoring was achieved with a school-level national assessment which led to additional support to improve the quality of the learning environment, including school rehabilitation, and water and sanitation facilities. The Back-to-School Initiative has continued in 2003 with the provision of educational materials to 4 million children. The role of education in national reconstruction was clearly demonstrated, with the challenge now to sustain and extend such unprecedented success.

6.4.9. Supporting Rural Ethnic Minority Girls in Viet Nam

Viet Nam's net primary school enrolment rate is over 90%, which is an impressive achievement given the country's low GNP/capita. However, one-third of children do not complete grade 5 and 70% of dropouts are girls. Moreover, the overall impressive performance masks significant disparities. A tour of the primary schools in ethnic minority areas of the rural north reveals very few girls in class. UNICEF supports the government's work in primary education for ethnic minority children through multigrade classes, satellite schools and in-service teacher training.

In 2002, UNICEF provided a package of strategic interventions designed to boost girls' enrolments in selected districts, communes and communities. This benefited more than 9,000 disadvantaged girls, particularly girls of ethnic minorities. Capacity-building has focused on the development of training modules for teachers (Gender and Child Rights and Multi-Grade Teaching techniques); principals (Better School Management); and Parent-Teacher Associations and Education Councils (Community Partnerships in Education). Initial training for selected parents, teachers and principals has focused on how to promote girls' enrolment and completion. UNICEF also initiated a monitoring system to encourage community partnership in monitoring of education achievements through 'COMPAS', a database on children and women in education. Results so far show that enrolment trends for girls in the project areas are improving, however, they remain below the national average, indicating the need for continued efforts.

6.4.10. Child-friendly Schools through the African Girls' Education Initiative (AGEI)

In Africa, generally low overall education indicators are compounded by disparities based on gender, poverty and rural/ urban location. Data from recent household surveys in 36 countries in sub-Saharan Africa reveal that only 52% of rural children attend primary school, compared to 73% of urban children, with such disparities associated with high levels of rural poverty. In six of the countries sampled more than 7 out of 10 rural children were not attending school. Within the urban/rural disparities, girls are often the most deprived, as shown on the accompanying figures showing comparative net primary school attendance rates (NAR) for selected countries in Eastern & Southern Africa and Western & Central Africa.

Some 34 countries across Africa are currently participating in UNICEF's African Girls' Education Initiative (AGEI), initiated in 1994 with support from Canada and continued from 1996 with generous support from Norway. Through the rich experiential knowledge base and successful models it has built, AGEI is helping to consolidate and extend support to 'child-friendly schools' incorporating multiple dimensions of access and quality with a strong gender component. A strong partnership with the Forum of African Women Educationalists (FAWE) has strengthened implementation and advocacy around this initiative. A number of programmes include a particular focus on rural areas.

6.4.11. Satellite Schools and Early Learning Centres in Burkina Faso

In Burkina Faso, survey results reveal that only a fifth of school age children in rural areas are attending school, compared to nearly three quarters in urban areas. Among rural girls, the net attendance rate drops to 15%. UNICEF supports a network of satellite schools in under-served rural areas in an effort to bring schools closer—both physically and culturally—to children's milieu. Inspired by the BRAC model in Bangladesh and the Escuela Nueva approach in Latin America, the accent is on relevant curricula that responds to local realities; recruitment of local teachers; initial mother tongue instruction to ease the transition to French; enhanced community participation in school management and use of facilities; and intersectoral linkages through appropriate water and sanitation facilities in schools, school canteens, and accompanying support for early child care and development centres. These latter, known as 'bisongo' help ensure that young children have a good start to education and also free up older girls from the care of their younger siblings so that they can, in turn, attend school. Since 1995, some 230 satellite schools have been constructed and equipped with furniture and double latrines, with assessments showing positive results in attitudes, enrolments and learning achievement. Satellite schools are now inscribed in the 10-year development plan for basic education and in UNICEF's acceleration strategy for girls' education.

6.4.12. Innovations and Intersectoral Synergy in Guinea

In Guinea, the 'Ecole Milieu' approach aims at fostering a new type of school in rural areas with low enrolment among girls, including through relevant curricula and enhanced community participation. Complementary efforts to bridge the gap between school and family include development of a 'school monitoring file' which allows parents and teachers to more closely follow their children's progress, while non-formal education centres (known as 'Nafa' centres) help extend educational opportunities to children and adolescents who are outside of the formal system. Intersectoral synergy to maximise the impact of education initiatives is pursued through partnerships with, for example, the World Food Programme (school canteens; food rations to parents of girls), while the multi-partner FRESH initiative is being implemented on an experimental basis in 30 schools.

6.4.13. Boarding Schools in Botswana and Education against HIV/AIDS

In Botswana, according to a 1997 assessment, some 47% of the population lives below the poverty line, with rural areas the worst affected. In partnership with government and other organisations, UNICEF has been involved in improving the boarding school environment for children living in remote areas where girls' and boys' enrolment is low. A project for remote area dwellers in the district with the highest rate of out-ofschool girls was implemented in partnership with the Ministry of Education, local NGOs, local authorities, and the private sector. The project has influenced hostel design. Given the magnitude of the HIV/AIDS crisis in Botswana, which is undermining national efforts to promote and protect the rights of children and women, UNICEF is now focusing national support on Improvement of Schools as Child Friendly, Community Outreach Centers for HIV/AIDS Resources and Services, including through the development of life skills packages and peer education programmes.

6.4.14. Green, Clean and Healthy Schools in Mauritania

In Mauritania, where poverty is concentrated among rural populations, there is a strong link between the level of instruction and the degree of poverty. Rates of retention are particularly low among girls, with poverty, the gender-division of labour, early marriage, and discriminatory attitudes and practices among the key contributing factors. The national Poverty Reduction Strategy emphasises the strengthening of basic social services, including education, in the areas of greatest need. UNICEF supports a community-based multi-sectoral approach to education through the Green, Clean and Healthy school project which has been piloted in 120 sites. Targeting schools in both peri-urban and rural areas, the project includes the construction of hand-washing facilities and separate toilets for boys and girls, provision of gender-sensitive school manuals, tree-planting activities and school gardens. Other aspects include stronger community participation in school management and monitoring, social mobilisation around girls' education, and development of cultural and athletic opportunities for girls. Positive results have been registered in enrolment rates, community attitudes to girls' education and hygiene practices and conditions in both schools and the surrounding villages. The approach has been adopted for wider application within the government's national education development programme.

6.4.15. Quality education in Uganda

All scientific evidence points to the crucial importance of the early childhood years in the social, psychological, and cognitive growth of a child. Yet information and support services for parents and organised early childhood development activities and pre-schools are often lacking—particularly in rural areas. UNICEF's child-friendly basic education and learning programme in Uganda includes support for the development of integrated early childhood development services and child-friendly schools in priority districts, with an emphasis on lower primary education. Cost-effective models developed at household, community/ cluster, and district level help link child survival, growth and development, with a focus on convergence of services and interventions. At national level, a learning framework for early childhood development has been developed and used as a training module for parents and teachers in focus districts.

Child-friendly schools in ten districts emphasise the importance of girls' education at lower primary level, as well as the inclusion of un-reached children and children affected by HIV/AIDS. The 'break-through to literacy' programme has been identified as a best practice for early learning and life-skills, with equal achievements among girls and boys. The Girls' Education Movement (GEM) empowers girls as leaders and boys as strategic allies to help identify out-of- school children and draw them in. Intersectoral synergies are sought in a number of schools through support for the multi-partner FRESH initiative (Focussing Resources for effective school Health) which provides for the provision of appropriate water and sanitation facilities, the training of teachers in skills-based health education, and school-based health and nutrition services.

Meanwhile, through the use of innovative techniques and flexible timetables, the Alternative Basic Education Programme for Karamoja (ABEK) is extending educational opportunities to children of pastoral, seminomadic communities of northeastern Uganda, while the Complementary Opportunities for Primary Education (COPE) is being implemented in 8 districts where disadvantaged children have remained outside of the formal school system.

References

Abu-Ghaida, D. and S. Klasen, "The Costs of Missing the Millennium Development Goal on Gender Equity," *World Development*, Vol. 32, No. 7., Elsevier: Great Britain: 2004.

Abu-Ghaida and Klasen, and N. Mellington and L. Cameron, "Female Education and Child Mortality," *Bulletin of Indonesian Economic Studies*, Vol.35, No.3, 1999.

Anderlini, S.N., *Women at the Peace Table: Making a Difference*, UNIFEM: New York: 2000.

Behrman J., A. Foster, M. Rosenzweig and P.Vashishthe, "Women's Schooling, Home Teaching, and Economic Growth," *Journal of Political Economy*, Vol.107, No.4, 1999.

Brock, C. and Cammish, N.K., "Factors affecting female participation in education in seven developing countries," *DIFID Education*, London: DIFID, Serial No. 9, 1997.

Cammish, N. and Brock, C., "Girls, Schools and Limits to Change", *ID21 Society and Economy*, 4 March 1999.

CERID, "Promotion of Girls' Education", *Through Recruitment and Training of Female Teachers in Nepal: A country case study*, Kathmandu: Center for Educational Research, Innovation and Development, 1996.

Frost, G., "Learning the value of girls education, Oxfam. Sa Pa, Viet Nam, 1999.

Maimbolwa-Sinyangwe, I. M. and B.Y. Chilangwa, "Learning from Inside the Classroom: A research report", UNICEF/Ministry of Education, Zambia, December 1995.

United Nations Children's Fund, *The State of the World's Children 2003*, UNICEF, New York, 2002.

UN Millennium Project, Task Force on Education and Gender Equality, *Toward Universal Primary Education: Investments, Incentives, and Institutions*, Earthscan: London/Sterling,VA: 2005.

UNESCO, *EFA Global Monitoring Report 2003-04, Gender and Education for All:The Leap to Equality*, Paris: 2003.

________________ , *Women and Girls: Education, Not Discrimination*, New York: 2000.

________________ , *Gender and Education for All: The Leap to Equality: Summary Report*, Paris: 2003.

7

Education for Eradicating Rural Poverty

About two thirds of India's more than 1 billion people live in rural areas, and almost 170 million of them are poor. Although many rural people are migrating to cities, three out of four of India's poor people live in the vast rural parts of the country. For more than 21 per cent of them, poverty is a chronic condition.

A major cause of poverty among rural people in India is lack of access for both individuals and communities to productive assets and financial resources. High levels of illiteracy, inadequate health care and extremely limited access to social services are common among poor rural people. Microenterprise development, which could generate income and enable them to improve their living conditions, has only recently become a focus of the government.

Current health and education programmes have less outreach to rural areas, yet rural people have lower health and literacy. Other things equal, higher rural outlay should raise productivity more than higher urban outlay. Rural anti-poverty policy is centred on increasing productivity, often with success. But much urban anti-poverty policy concentrates on improving the poor's shelter and sanitation rather than their chance to earn incomes. Rural cost-per-job of infrastructure and direct investment is usually less. The main rural activity (agriculture) rewards scale or capital-intensity. This is not true of urban industry and modern services. However, the dispersion of rural public action, and hence high management costs, could offset the productivity advantages of rural public spending.

7.1. Rural-urban Interactions

Extra urban work chances encourage migration from rural to

urban areas. Congestion costs will rise, and the wages of the urban poor may fall. Conversely, irrigation and improved seeds can push down staples prices, yet push down non-labour costs of staples cultivation on smallholdings faster. Then—whether among small farmers, farmworkers, or urban food buyers—the very poor, who spend most of their incomes on food staples, benefit. There is no corresponding urban output which, by being expanded or made cheaper, enriches the rural poor. The most cost-effective way to cut urban poverty may be to cut rural poverty.

7.2. Rural-to-urban Migration

This is, in part, a way of sharing risk by families that maintain rural and urban households, often shifting members between them. But risks must also be taken, and initial costs incurred, for rural-to-urban migration. The poorest can rarely undertake it, certainly not in a single step. Unequal, rather than low-income, villages have high rates of rural-to-urban migration, with moderately poor people 'pushed' and moderately well-off people 'pulled'; but neither the richest nor the poorest are very likely to urbanise permanently.

Countries with very unequal assets, and perhaps income, usually experience slower economic growth. This matters for the choice between rural and urban poverty reduction, in two ways. First, some inequality of reward seems necessary to create incentives for effort, achievement, or meeting effective demand seems necessary to generate incentives. But inequality that reflects ascribed position, status, or inheritance reduces earned incomes, and creates barriers to the advancement of efficient and able persons. This happens when more or better schools, clinics, prices, or research inputs are assigned to persons who happen to be born in towns. Second, inequality is especially likely to deter growth if it concentrates resources in large units of production with economies of scale—normally absent in farming; concentrating anti-poverty resources on the rural poor in small farms is likely to promote both efficiency and equality. In short, greatly expanding resources for reducing rural poverty would be justified by its persistently greater incidence and depth as compared with towns, and the apparently higher returns to rural anti-poverty policy.

7.3. Effective Poverty Reduction Strategies

The rural and the poor are usually late to enjoy the changes that cut fertility: better prospects for child survival, girls' education, women's work. So the gains from fertility transition (fewer poverty-increasing deaths and births; later, rising worker/dependent ratios) arrive later for the rural and poor, unless policy speeds them up.

For the poor to gain much, their extra potential workers and savings must be matched by extra, attractive chances for work and investment, as in E/SE Asia. In other words, realising the huge potential for reducing poverty, especially rural poverty, in the ongoing demographic revolution is a matter of policy to empower rural people to choose rapid mortality and fertility transitions: better child health and nutrition, readier access to contraception, improved work and school chances for women. Policy and institutional structures must become more pro-rural and pro-poor if the rural poor are to experience the huge overall rises in worker/dependant ratios as personal paths out of poverty.

Effective poverty reduction requires resource reallocations to the rural and the poor:

- Big rural income, poverty, nutrition/health and education gaps are not closing. Though rural poverty fell sharply in 1970-85, the decline has slowed; it bypassed countries, ethnic and other groups, and whole regions and agro-ecologies.

  Addressing rural poverty raises food supply, may reduce migration, and thus helps reduce urban poverty. Also, successful rural poverty reduction usually works by raising the productivity of the poor; but most treatments of urban poverty are welfare-oriented, often depending mainly on upgraded housing.

- Poverty reduction and asset equalisation, especially in rural areas, assist growth. Ongoing big rises in worker/child ratios provide a 'window of opportunity' for poverty reduction—but only if the extra adults find attractive yet affordable work. To that end, the rural poor need to share much more in the female empowerment, and better health and education, that permit fertility decline; and in research, investment, and employment for the working poor.

Yet aid, even more than public investment, goes disproportionately to countries -and increasingly to non-rural sectors—where most of the poor do not live or work.

7.3.1. Declining the Prices of Farm Products

Declines in the role of agriculture and the rural sector in supporting and advancing people, especially the poor, in low-income countries. Such declines are: surprisingly small even as measured; partly spurious; with least impact on the poorest; and, to benefit the poor as in Asia, usually dependent on demand from prior staples-based growth.

Indeed, part of the case for public support for poor people's farming is that private support, e.g. for research and infrastructure [even where not public goods], is systematically undersupplied due to pass-on of many gains to private consumers from whom (as from small farmers themselves) support costs are not readily recoverable. To keep private rates up [i.e. prevent artificial depression of world farm prices], do not hobble aid and support for small/poor farms in labour-surplus areas, but (a) concentrate them on smallholdings/labour-intensives, so most income gain reaches the poor, who use much of it to buy farm products, so the price-depressing effect is less; (b) while recognising the frequent primacy of 9 staples production in early development, shift 'up-market' to farm products with more income-elastic demand (livestock, horticulture) as incomes grow; (c) phase out subsidies inducing oversupply by large/rich farmers (in rich countries and poor).

7.3.2. Aid Fungibility

At the mean of all variable values, past rises in the share of aid for the average sector seems to bring offsetting public expenditure-share cuts there. First, however, this is unlikely to apply where the aid/public investment ratio is far above the mean; donors finance 30-50% or more of public investment in sub-Saharan Africa and much of Latin America. Second, agriculture may not be an 'average sector' and fungibility may not work both ways: governments may not have responded to lost agricultural aid by increasing domestically-financed public agriculture investment. Third, remedies for fungibility often post-date fungibility research. Fourth, substituting aid investment for domestic subsidy is no bad thing. Fifth, the research relates to sector aid fungibility, but agriculture aid is also supposed to bring gains by changing the project-mix; the record of aid-induced agricultural research supports this.

7.3.3. Assets and Rural Poverty Reduction

Assets can empower the rural poor by increasing their income, reserves against shocks, and choices to escape from harsh or exploitative conditions. Urban-rural and rich-poor gaps in asset ownership far exceed the gaps in income and consumption, making the rural poor specially dependent on unsupported labour power. Assets most help rural poverty reduction when they are employment intensive, divisible into small low-cost units, and low-risk. For many important assets gender bias doubly harms the poor: as a source of injustice to children and women; and as a source of inefficiency and slow growth.

There are strong complementarities among asset types. The poor (and economic growth) do better with some improvement in health, nutrition and schooling than with a lot in one and none for the others. Human assets do more for a poor person if she also has some farm assets whose productivity is rising. Previous education helps a poor person get better returns from irrigation. Participation in designing and implementing public asset policy—locating wells, running schools—helps both efficiency and poverty reduction.

Extreme land inequality is bad for growth, and steers its benefits away from the rural poor. Most of them depend on farm income, yet, except in parts of West Africa and South America, usually control little farmland. Land reform to create small, not-too unequal family farms is often cost-effective in reducing beneficiary poverty; in one important study the welfare 'impact was several [times] greater than that of education', and most for the poorest. It also helps hired farmworkers; small farms employ more people per hectare than do large farms, and small farmers and their employees spend more of their incomes on employment-intensive rural non-farm products. Redistribution of farmland to the poor has been substantial and successful in many areas; is continuing; and leaves small farms usually at least as productive as large.

However, post-reform farmers, to escape poverty sustainably, need appropriate infrastructures and services; these needs change with liberalisation and globalisation. Also, some past land reform has been unduly confiscatory, statist or top-down. 'New-wave land reform' is sometimes feasible and consistent with property rights. But getting land assets to the poor should avoid imposing particular modes of tenure, and should recognise that many households, laws and customs discriminate against women—harming efficiency, equity, child health and poverty reduction. There is a strong case for increased support, by governments and donors, for farmland redistribution to poor communities, households and women.

Extreme land inequality's impact on overall inequality does not appear to diminish even when agriculture's role does. So land redistribution remains cost-effective against poverty in Latin America and Southern Africa. There, some ethnic groups remain specially prone to rural poverty, largely due to exceptional inequality of farmland as well as education.

Some water control is essential for full benefits from farmland. East and South Asia's fast poverty reduction and farm growth owe much to the 30-35 per cent of irrigated farmland—and the persistence of rural poverty and agricultural stagnation in most of sub-Saharan Africa, to its mere 1-5 per cent. Water control is also vital for adequate and healthy drinking-water and sanitation. Yet the rural and the poor have even less access to water-yielding assets, and hence water control, than to land and face growing water stress. Improving this depends partly on redistributing water-yielding assets, and on incentives for asset types that save water by using labour. Small, divisible, farmer-controlled water supply systems benefit the poor most, but in some conditions and with environmental caution, large systems remain essential. In either case, user participation in design, management and maintenance are proven keys to asset efficiency, yet are usually absent. Special attention to women's water rights is needed.

Women and children are also the main losers from distant, inadequate and unhealthy drinking water. Modest but enforced water charges (payable as maintenance labour), complementary water improvement and health care, and managed credit to acquire water-yielding assets are keys to pro-poor and efficient use of increasingly scarce rural water, for production or consumption.

Rural non-farm activity provides 25-40 per cent of rural income—sometimes more for the poor, sometimes less—and is outpacing farm income. But its dynamism usually depends on demand from a growing, fairly equal farm sector. Diverting resources from poor farmers and farmworkers, to advance the non-farm poor, is self-defeating. Usually, the poor, the rural, and the rural poor are specially deprived of 'human assets'—health, child nutrition, education, skills. In the medium term, these are the most effective, just and growth-inducing ways to advance the rural poor—provided there are also physical assets, or work , yielding more to the educated, in a growing economy.

More and better health, education and nutrition normally induce each other, are complementary, and if acquired by mothers, benefit children. Usually provision and quality discriminate heavily and inefficiently against rural areas, remote places, ethnic minorities, and (in education) women. Such discrimination is most severe among the poor. Of human assets, primary schooling and health care for the poor must long be financed mainly by the public sector. Financial viability and participatory management are real problems. But user fees in primary health and education are not the answer. They have proved very hard to target correctly; have saved little public money; and have discouraged service use by the rural poor and hence growth of their incomes. Other ways to financial viability and participation for human asset provision are feasible.

7.3.4. Role of Technology and Natural Resources

Technology is central in reducing rural poverty. Rice, wheat and maize, in much of Asia and Central America, in 1965-85 experienced a big employment-enhancing, yield-increasing technology shift, and a rapid fall in poverty.

But yield growth, employment effect and poverty impact have slowed. Technical progress has by-passed hundreds of millions of poor people—many of the remaining hard-core poor—in specific regions (including most of Africa), agroecologies (dry/upland), and products (millet, smallstock).

Poverty reduction and natural-resource sustainability can be harmed by inappropriate or stagnant technology. Without technical progress in well-watered lands, farmers are induced to grow staples intensively on marginal hill and semi-arid lands, depleting them further and faster.

Recent scientific advance can—but as currently financed and organised probably will not—re-ignite, and spread to laggard areas and crops, poverty-reducing, resource-conserving technical change:-

1. The 1965-85 green revolution was led by non-profit institutions. Today, agricultural research is concentrated in a few firms, which patent or physically protect results. Profit incentives direct them to meet demand from well-off food consumers, processors and farmers, not calorie or employment needs of the poor.
2. Progress in tropical food staples has largely come from new crop varieties. Land and water management technology have advanced slowly, with less progress in basic science, yet are essential for natural-resource conservation.
3. Formal researchers still engage too little with the priorities, knowledge, research and multi-source livelihoods of poor farmers (let alone labourers)—most serious for 'complex, diverse, risk-prone' dry or hilly farm systems.

In bio-agricultural research, it is imperative to restore the thrust towards enhanced yield potential (and yield growth in 'lead' areas) and to spread progress to neglected regions and main staples. Both present major but soluble problems. They require sharp reversal of the long fall in levels (and security) of funds for public-sector agricultural research—and of the growing diffusion of such research systems, often at the behest of donors, into matters other than yield enhancement, stabilisation and sustainability. Also needed is more public-sector research into transgenic staples, with traits prioritised by labour-intensive smallholders. This requires new incentives for research, now increasingly directed towards traits, crops, and farmers of little interest to the poor.

Transgenic crops and animals have triggered justified public demand for open, publicly participatory systems, effectively regulating food safety and environmental impact of introduced varieties, species and foods. To realise the huge potential progress from transgenics, especially for areas hitherto little affected by research, requires big changes in the criteria and incentives now guiding the allocation, use, and civil-society overview of scientific resources. Public/private, and donor-agency/civilsociety, partnership action is urgent, especially for those developing counties with limited scientific capacity, yet heavily dependent on food staples yield growth.

Inaction in this field, and in parallel areas of agricultural and water technology, could undermine all other efforts for rural poverty reduction in coming decades. Improved land management technology has proved slow to spread, or improve farm income; ill-integrated with bio-agricultural research; yet vital to reduce land depletion. Such technology, to attract poor farmers, needs to show production returns. It should employ labour (preferably slack-season) rather than equipment. In these respects some forms of conservation tillage and land reclamation have proved far better than others. Technical choices are crucial to meeting the water crisis that increasingly threatens many rural poor.

Agriculture is being pressed in most developing countries to 'use' less water, but water used need not be used up. Employment-intensive ways to improve conveyance and use efficiency have proved feasible, with proper incentives and user institutions. However, justified emphasis on farmers' methods of water control has distracted attention from the need for faster progress in this area with formal, 'frontier' invention and innovation suitable for smallholders.

7.3.5. Globalised Markets

Markets benefit the rural poor to the extent that they are (a) open, on a fair basis, to rural groups (remote dwellers, women, ethnic minorities) especially prone to poverty or exclusion; (b) adequate to connect buyers with sellers—of products, consumables, factors (like land, water or labour), and facilitators (like credit)—at reasonable transport and transaction costs, and with minimal missing, wrong or asymmetric information; monopoly or monopsony power; or market failure (e.g. if some producers can costlessly pollute water for others).

Liberalisation and globalisation have enormously increased the importance of markets for many rural poor, usually increasing opportunity and income but also fluctuation and risk; but they have bypassed others, too distant, roadless, or otherwise disadvantaged to enjoy access. Most of the rural poor are substantially involved in markets for labour, consumed food, farm and non-farm inputs, and often credit. Liberalisation, since 1980, has increased gains from trade, but poor people and remote places face very high physical and transactions costs of marketing, restricting trade, specialisation and growth.

Villagers themselves give priority to road access. Yet in remote and sparsely populated areas, with little potential surplus to exchange, roadbuilding cost per beneficiary, and per unit of potential extra output, is large. In such areas, better road maintenance, more appropriate vehicles, swifter information, improved storage of perishables, higher value/weight ratios of produce, or improved communications can be more cost-effective than paved roads in enlarging markets and reducing poverty. Also, gains from market access and liberalisation are both greater and easier to achieve where assets (bicycles, schooling) are less unequally distributed.

The market access problems of particular groups (e.g. the illiterate) are distinct from problems of remote areas. In each case, problems of physical access (e.g. bad or no roads) are distinct from transaction-costs of, or bias in, institutional market access (e.g. trader or marketing-board monopsony). Often, problems interact: women, and indigenous ethnic minorities in both Asia and Africa, are likelier to be remote dwellers; bad roads are linked to trader monopsony. But resources can be saved by deciding at the start which problem—or mix of problems—is tackled most cost-effectively, to achieve a given poverty reduction through better rural market access.

Almost everywhere, remote and ill-connected rural people are poorer. If they have few potential tradable surpluses, then generating these, usually through better farm technology, is a precondition for generating exchange and cutting poverty through better roads. If an area feeds itself adequately but lacks transport links, these are usually needed to make yield-enhancing staples technology attractive. For cash crops or non-farm products, better roads are usually needed to permit expansion, marketing, and growth through specialisation. There are many cases of poor non-remote people -separated by terrain, not distance, from nearby markets—whose welfare increased greatly when such markets allowed trade and exchange. Even if such people have roads, but no bus or bicycle, their lack of choice, especially for small transactions, can expose them to large transactions- or institutional costs.

Private traders and parastatal marketing boards expose the poor to non-contestable market power (the non-poor can more readily find alternatives). Yet withdrawal of parastatals or monopsony traders often leaves the rural poor stranded altogether. Marketing co-operatives are a decentralised solution, depending for success on acceptance as 'institutions of trust' or so-called social capital. Regulated markets, overseeing adulteration, weights and market-rigging, have been a successful top-down approach in parts of India. Overall, improving market institutions is often a necessary complement to liberalisation, if the effect of better prices on poor rural people is not to be swamped by marketing costs.

Commercialisation—a rising ratio of exchange to self-provisioning—usually improves the welfare of the poor. Being intelligently risk-averse, they avoid premature commitment to all the risks of commercialisation, e.g. keeping part of their land for self-provisioning. Indeed, cash-crop income is often used to acquire improved staples technology. Crop diversification is another risk-diffusing strategy, but rapid change is often not practicable, e.g. with tree crops.

Access to transparent input markets is crucial for the poor. It is self-defeating to substitute, for land asset redistribution, measures that lead to missing, hidden, or distorted tenancy markets. Water markets almost always favour the poor more than non-price water rationing and subsidy, which usually target the non-poor and leave the poor with the distortion costs. Rural user fees for water (unlike primary education/health) are usually pro-poor; a tightening rural water squeeze may make water pricing essential on efficiency grounds.

New farm technology is sometimes embodied in costly capital confined to the betteroff (e.g. deep tubewells), but has often been distributed free, as information -sometimes alongside free or subsidised seed or seed-fertiliser packages—through extension. Returns have often been high; but in Africa most public extension services are in disarray (and may have little of value to extend), while in Latin America extension (like research) is increasingly privatised, even for the poor. New market or other routes to reduce the time-lag before adoption of better technologies by the poor are badly needed, if the poor are not to miss out on new opportunities.

In labour markets, discrimination against ethnic minorities, women, and scheduled castes and tribes, though usually illegal, is common. It works less by specific wage-rates than by exclusion from high-productivity tasks or places: through lack of education and skills; women's domestic 'duties' that restrict tasks; and remoteness and language for ethnic minorities. Rural public works can powerfully enhance access. The poor are restricted by asymmetric information (and high unit costs) from most formal credit, and (given the covariance of local loans) by lack of collateral from much moneylender lending. Efforts to reach the rural poor through directed, subsidised statebacked credit largely failed. The current approach is to generate unsubsidised, but nonexploitative, micro-finance markets through local peer-monitored intermediation, with NGO-based lenders like Grameen Bank in Bangladesh. This has had considerable success, but outreach to the very poor may conflict with financial sustainability.

Markets for the rural poor are being restructured by trade liberalisation and globalisation. This removes biases against farm prices, raising food production and employment but also food prices, with ambiguous effects on the poor. Economic growth should normally benefit them in the long run, as should labour-intensive specialisation. However, such gains can be destroyed by bad market transmission and functioning. Remote areas, benefiting (despite its gross inefficiencies) from panterritorial pricing, have lost out where subsidies have been removed, and where the parastatal has been withdrawn and not replaced by competing private buyers.

Though the poor on the whole gain from liberalisation, substantial and desperate groups often lose, and need compensation. People with little education, few roads or contacts, or speaking a minority language, are specially likely to be 'stuck' as immobile losers. Conversely, reasonably equal access to markets—and to asset control—greatly help the poor to gain quickly from liberalisation: for example, great land inequalities mean that higher food prices penalise many of the rural poor as net food buyers, rather than benefiting them through extra farm income. Liberalisation—while probably raising long-run GDP and, at worst, not lowering the rural poor's share of it—often increases income fluctuations, especially from export crops. Access to quasi-insurance or safety-nets therefore becomes important, if the poor are to realise secure gains from trade.

Small farms are generally efficient and employment-intensive, globalisation means new strains—and prospects. It links product sales—especially in the booming horticultural sector, in principle ideal for small labour-intensive farms—increasingly to exports to rich countries and to supermarkets, abroad and at home. This exposes farmers to a range of unfamiliar requirements, from uniform product appearance, through pesticide rules, to restrictions on child labour. The cost per unit of output, both of meeting these requirements for farmers and of supervising them for buyers, is initially much higher on small farms. Such agricultural globalisation can undermine their economic advantages. To stimulate and support institutional remedies may be vital to a pro-poor trajectory.

7.3.6. Role of Institutions and Organisations

The distribution of benefits depends on institutions: organisations such as banks, and rules (customary or legal) such as those affecting division of inherited land, or the shares of landlord and tenant. Some acceptance of institutionally mediated outcomes is essential; but, unless institutions can change under pressure, a society's outcomes are 'frozen' in the interests of the existing controllers of the institutions. This favours the rural poor only if they control the institutions, or at least can compel attention to their needs from those who do.

Yet institutions are created and run in the interests of the powerful. These may come under political, economic or ethical pressure to benefit the poor, from the poor themselves or otherwise. But on the whole the powerful will run—or allow the poor to help run—pro-poor institutions only if they expect to gain (or to avoid loss) by so doing. This is a harder problem for institutional reform seeking to help the rural poor: if centralised, because of urban government, concentration, power, and bias; if decentralised, because that puts the determination of institutional outcomes into the hands of rural 'big men'—and the rural gap between big and small (and men and women) is huge as regards literacy, information and other prerequisites of political success. That rural big men run local institutions in their interest is the problem for top-down institutional devolution, decentralisation and participation.

However, institutions usually respond—whether by revolution or by evolution—to reduce inefficiencies that, by reducing output and income, hurt everyone. Institutions are amended to ease production with plentiful rather than scarce resources, and to reduce the costs of transactions, which can rapidly change in type during development.

Decentralised institutions for natural resource management and financial services rarely help the rural poorest 'directly' but often reach the moderately poor, and help all through increased efficiency and sustainability, as the locally powerful are driven to recognise their shared interests with the poor in these. Privatisation too proved inefficient and unequal. Participatory decentralisation became a growing trend. Where consultation and information systems were built with care (and delay and cost)—and where user groups were small, fairly homogeneous (or very unequal), with a history of mutual trust, and with clearly demarcated property rights—decentralised natural-resource management has improved on the state's record in conservation and efficiency—but less often in the poor's share of benefits. To enlist the poor in natural-resource conservation, the methods must not require them to invest for the distant future at the cost of essential consumption now, and must contribute to their livelihoods or security, as with vegetative bunds.

Untrammelled markets, too, did not adequately reach even the creditworthy poor. Hence micro-financing agencies, usually lending without subsidy to small groups of borrowers with joint liability, and often providing deposit and other financial services, were widely attempted, often with NGO support, and often targeted on women and on non-farm lending. In respect of sustainability, repayment, and outreach to the moderately poor, it greatly improves on most previous public and private rural credit—yet it, too, seldom reaches the poorest. Their risk-proneness and complex, fluctuating household economies require a wider range of financial services, often at high unit cost, centred on consumption smoothing (e.g. insurance) rather than micro-enterprise support.

For success, poor people's groups need options and voice; hence the importance of a reserve of land, and of literacy and political openness. The dilemma of 'willing participation from above' is increasingly softened, if not solved, by partnerships involving donors, governments and NGOs. But careful selection—of governments, NGOs and projects—is essential for cost-effective gains to the rural poor.

7.3.7. Better Education for Poor

Quality education is a gateway to prosperity in later life, yet many children in the world do not have access to that education. It matters greatly where you are born. A child born in a rich country has a very high chance of being literate as an adult. In a poor country, the chance is considerably smaller.

The World Declaration on Education for All, Article I states that "Every person—child, youth and adult—shall be able to benefit from educational opportunities designed to meet their basic learning needs. These needs comprise both essential learning tools (such as literacy, oral expression, numeracy, and problem solving) and the basic learning content required by human beings to be able to survive, to develop their full capacities, to live and work in dignity, to participate fully in development, to improve the quality of their lives, to make informed decisions, and to continue learning." Reaching all types of learners in an education system cannot be left to chance.

When providing the poor with appropriate education, there are fundamental objectives to be addressed, including the need to:

a) increase productivity, i.e., improving their work output
b) support more efficient yet ecologically sensitive use of the natural environment

c) provide essential knowledge on how to improve access to socio-economic resources and ensure social well-being through various communication channels
d) improve traditional technologies and introduce new ones
e) ensure that children remain literate when they leave school
f) encourage self-reliance, initiative and enterprise

Scholarships, welfare support and targeted interventions have had some impact on the lives of the poor. Although individuals have benefited, they have not altered the way education systems function: The path to progress in education has to be charted, and success carefully monitored. Target groups have to be clearly defined and their culture and aspirations understood by those, who plan for or- with them. The planners need to know where the poor are located and reach out to them, starting with captive audiences such as children in formal and non-formal education, poor houses and asylums, rnicro-credit borrowers and members of co-operatives.

A gender-sensitive education system must also provide opportunities for women to receive short term training to meet the immediate needs of industries. For example, when governments negotiate the establishment of export industries, training programmes should be set up for women, not only to train them in the skills which they need, but also in ways of protecting their rights in the labour force. New jobs are being created in technology and women need to be trained in order to obtain these jobs. In short, education systems should be alert to potential job opportunities for women and help to prepare them to access such opportunities.

In an age of information technology and the global liberation of knowledge, there is no need for women to wait until they are literate in order to become self reliant. It is the task of education to find appropriate ways and means of providing women with essential knowledge. Modem technology makes it possible for this knowledge to be acquired in their own environment. Imaginative ways will be needed to find the resources and to make such technology feasible and affordable. For the purpose of poverty eradication, youth programmes need to be given high priority. Community centres that offer vocational training, recreational activities and useful information are urgently needed in developing countries.

In addition to job creation, young people need to learn skills in citizenship and how to manage their leisure time. Guidance and counselling services should be available to all young people and especially to those who are "at risk" of drug abuse, prostitution, adolescent pregnancy, HIV/AIDS and other social evils. Youths can and will help themselves if there is an enabling environment.

7.3.8. Integrating Health and Education

Most education systems are centrally planned and administered and are narrowly focused on academic achievement geared to progress through educational levels. Those children who do not fit into this educational ladder do not succeed in the system. The time has come for education systems to develop a more dynamic planning approach. Educational plans should include poor children's primary health and welfare. This calls for a more integrated approach with other sectors and should be addressed on two fronts. It should incorporate health knowledge and behaviour in the learning programme as well as the provision of health care at the places of learning. Education can further contribute to children's health through the interaction of educational institutions (whether formal or non-formal) with communities so that they become a focal point for community health.

There are common deficiencies which can be addressed within the school system by teachers and health workers, and which should be identified and addressed in educational development programmes. For example, it should be possible to implement the idea of 'health-promoting' schools by effective liaison between education and health professionals. This will require looking at all components of school programmes as part of a coherent strategy, rather than as isolated components. It is not suggested that education will assume the responsibility of other sectors, but rather that the sectors will complement each other and ensure that children are healthy and appropriately educated and informed on health-issues.

7.3.9. Interaction with Communities

Educational planning for all groups must necessarily include communities. Young people can be difficult to reach after they have left school, although informal and non-formal systems can devise effective strategies for so doing. The community, together with the school, can create a meeting place for them. Young people can be encouraged to see the school, not only as a centre for academic learning, but also as a place for community activities, sports, games and meetings. In this way the school becomes their place of assembly and they can be reached with meaningful assistance. This has substantial implications for the ways in which schools are managed and administered.

The collaboration between education and other sectors can be most effective in communities where there is a convergence of services. Educators, social workers, extension officers and health workers all converge in the same community and reach the same target group, and often address similar issues. It is important for community development that sectoral interests are brought together in an integrated whole, which can address better the economic and social concerns of the individual.

Education is sustained in an enabling environment. Libraries, reading kiosks and mobile reading services are all part of such an environment. These will make a significant contribution to the development of a society in which learning is valued for a wide variety of reasons, as well as being seen as a necessary part of overall personal and societal development.

7.3.10. Content of Education

Here, Articles 2 and 4 of the World Declaration on Education for All form an important point of departure. The former states, "To serve the basic learning needs of all requires more than a recommitment to basic education as it now exists. What is needed is an "expanded vision" that surpasses present resource levels, institutional structures, curricula, and conventional delivery systems while building on the 'best in current practices." The latter states "Whether or not expanded educational opportunities will translate into meaningful development—for an individual or for society- depends ultimately on whether people actually learn as a result of those opportunities, i.e., whether they incorporate useful knowledge, reasoning ability, skills and values."

When preparing the content of education, it is necessary to be able to understand the poor. More targeted research into social, political and economic skills will help educators to identify the content and scope of education. It will also be important to identify skills, values, attitudes and standards which the poor need in order to ensure their integration into the world at large. Education must go beyond literacy. It should seek to improve the learners' abilities to use available opportunities to "manipulate" the physical, social and economic environment so that they are prepared to create progress in their own societies.

Short term and long term educational planning strategies are needed to complement other efforts made to eradicate poverty. In the short term, the opportunities for learning among poor children who are already in the education system can be improved. The focus should be on appropriate content and methods in education, and the training of teachers to organise and conduct classes in which poor children are not disadvantaged. In the long term, education policies and programmes must be geared towards satisfying the learning needs of poor children, youths and adults.

The new directions must be reflected in the training of educational personnel and in the allocation of educational resources to poor areas and disadvantaged groups. It is time for education to recognise -the extent of the natural social and educational stimulation of young children living in poverty situations. Attempts are being made to identify the informal childcare practices that have been developed among the poor and to complement these with training materials. There is a renewed effort towards an integrated approach (care, health, nutrition and education) for enriching the developmental environment for the young. This approach has shown interesting results in Mexico, Bolivia, Chile and the Philippines. These programmes have also shown that the education of mothers in childcare practices has led to improved health care among children. These are good examples of the transformation of so-called deprivation into an active ingredient for educational achievement.

Most rural children start school at the age of six or seven years. By this time they have already had an education of their own in their families and communities. Some have already started to care for younger siblings and to contribute to family labour. Such education has content, methods, learning processes and evaluation as well as its own system of rewards and punishment. These are also features of a school education. A natural transition from their 'school' to the formal system improves their chances of success.

The children arrive at school with some concepts in all the subject areas of the curriculum for Grades 1 and 2. They know about the characteristics of living things, they know about force, pressure, small machines, light and heat. There is an urgent need to do more research into this education and to use its content and methodology as a starting point for Grades 1 and 2. The language of poor children is almost always different from the formal language of the school. If the spoken language is not completely different then it is a distortion of the official language. It is for the school system to bridge the two languages so that a poor child is able to use his or her own language in the early stage of schooling.

An approach to the identification of a curriculum which links the child's early learning experiences to Grades 1 and 2 can reduce the alien nature of the school and reduce drop outs in the early grades. Priority should be given in the early childhood years to good health and nutrition, socially balanced behaviour, and good parenting/child rearing practices within the context of the daily lives of families and communities. The renewed efforts to consider early childhood years beyond the confines of formally organised pre-schools to learning experiences for young children, is taking education even closer to equal opportunities for learning.

7.3.10.1. Education for personal development

In education, the affective domain is as important as the cognitive one. Over the years as classes have become larger in many countries, learners have been challenged to deal with and pass examinations. The affective domain has virtually disappeared from the learning environment but the escalation of social evils and civil unrest demands that the education system revitalise the teaching and learning of values. Co-operation, pride in a job well done, persistence, responsibility, curiosity, love of success, are among some of the values needed to help poor people to progress.

These are values that can be inculcated during a class in any subject.

7.3.10.2. *Promoting entrepreneurship*

Technical and vocational education and training opportunities linked to entrepreneurship and credit facilities can have a greater impact on learners. The exploration continues for suitable strategies to prepare young people in entrepreneurship skills. UNESCO International Project on Technical and Vocational Education (UNEVOC) is promoting a programme for entrepreneurial skill development in Asia-Pacific. Where possible, poor youths can be trained through contractual arrangements between governments and the private sector companies. The private sector makes substantial inputs to programme development and standard setting.

Special attention should be given to traditional community skills and the extent to which young people can improve them and make them economically viable. Many of these skills have been passed down from one generation to another and they give poor people the edge in productivity. The productive sector of society should be a key partner in developing such programmes, whether for school-age children or adults. Since there are not enough jobs in, the formal sector, special attention should be given to income generation in the informal sector. By the time some children get to school they have already been involved in informal trade, selling fruits, sweets, etc., for their parents. In many communities, this will continue to be a way of life. It is a responsibility of the education system to equip poor children, young people and adults to improve investment and returns for their efforts.

7.3.10.3. *Socio-economic Dimensions of Micro-credit System*

People world wide have tried to help themselves through informal monetary and micro-credit systems. Such funding has improved the lives of many, particularly women. However, the effectiveness of credit services can be improved if accompanied by an education designed to provide essential knowledge on health and education services, entrepreneurship, sources and use of knowledge, legislation and regulations, goal setting, and good communication etc.

Education will help poor people to maximise income from the credit and give them the potential to be heard. There are usually high illiteracy rates among micro-credit borrowers and often they are insufficiently informed about the areas in which they are involved. There is no need to wait to make them literate in order to provide access to important information. Appropriately sequenced and clear illustrations, videos, and tapes can provide information. Mobile resource boxes and resource centres can be established in their communities. Simultaneously literacy training should be provided using the same kind of information for those wishing to be literate.

References

Behrman, Jere R. and James C. Knowles, "Household Income and Child Schooling in Vietnam" *World Bank Economic Review,* 1999.

Datt, G. and M. Ravallion, "Farm Productivity and Rural Poverty In India", *Journal of Development Studies,* vol.34, no.4, 1998.

Datt, G. and M. Ravallion, "How Important to India's Poor is the Sectoral Composition of Economic Growth?' *The World Bank Economic Review,* vol.10, no.1, 1996.

Gaiha, R., "Poverty alleviation programs in rural India: an assessment", *Development and Change,* 1991.

Gaiha, R. & Kulkarni, V., "Is growth central to poverty alleviation in India?", *Journal of International Affairs,* 1998.

Ravallion, M. and G. Datt, "Farm Productivity and Rural Poverty in India", *Journal of Development Studies,* vol.34, no.4, 1998.

World Bank, *India- Poverty Reduction: Progress and Challenges,* Washington, D.C.World Bank: World Development Report, 2000.

8

Role of ICT in Rural Education

The evolution of information and communication technologies (ICTs) in India has created a technological divide between the 'haves' and the 'have-nots.' As many of India's companies and well-educated enjoy the benefits of ICTs, these technologies are still not accessible or affordable for the majority of the population. The divide is exacerbated by the deeply ingrained disparities of gender and social class, which determine who can or cannot use technology. Despite recent deregulation and decentralisation within India since the 1990s, which has strengthened the voice of the poor and the role of NGOs, there remains widespread poverty. Development initiatives, especially in rural areas, are hampered by weaknesses in technological infrastructure. Accessibility is also hindered by language barriers, and a lack of suitable content and applications in local languages.

Pan Asia's collaboration with the M.S. Swaminathan Research Foundation began in 1997, with the first phase of Impact of ICTs in Rural Areas. This phase aimed to assess and document the impact of ICTs in fostering sustainable agricultural and rural development and bridging the gap between the 'haves' and the 'have-nots.' During the first phase of the project, seven village knowledge centres (VKCs) were established in the rural areas of the Union Territory of Pondicherry. The second phase began in 2001, with additional funding from CIDA (Canadian International Development Agency), and has since established 4 more VKCs and deployed ICTs more widely throughout the region. The goal of this phase was to enhance connectivity in rural Pondicherry, and to assess the potential sustainability of the project.

The project used a hub-and-spokes model, whereby one village knowledge centre, operated by project staff, acts as a central hub for communication with the 11 other knowledge centres in surrounding villages as the spokes. Encouraging community ownership by involving the many local actors, including public and private partners and village volunteers, enhanced the project's sustainability. The programme challenged traditional gender roles by recruiting mainly women as volunteers for the centres. The project was designed to be non-discriminatory in its delivery of services, and provides relevant local information in Tamil language, both in written and verbal formats. As such, availability and accessibility for everyone is ensured.

A third phase of the project titled "Impact of ICTs on Poverty Alleviation in Rural Pondicherry" was approved in 2004, which focuses on ascertaining whether or not new, innovative ICTs can bring better economic sustainability to the existing project; while at the same time, contribute to further improvements in the education and health sector. The social and economic impacts of ICTs are assessed systematically through surveys, interviews, and participatory rural appraisal techniques to determine their effectiveness in poverty alleviation in rural Pondicherry.

This phase specifically utilises and assesses the following technologies: wireless fidelity (WiFi); 2.5G mobile technology (includes mobile telephones enabled to transmit data via General Packet Radio Service); Global Positioning System (GPS) for fisherpeople to improve knowledge of fishing zones and potential ocean hazards; Voice over Internet Protocol (VoIP) for low-cost long distance voice communication; and RailTel, a village network backbone via the Government of India-backed broadband network across India's railway networks.

Some of the ICT-based programmes being implemented in the villages include the development of an ICT-enabled integrated health system, computer-assisted learning centres for rural children, a multimedia indigenous knowledge directory for Pondicherry, a web-based information on food security, and a training course in knowledge management for local women. MSSRF is also experimenting with the use of open source software. The experience of this research project will be integrated into the National Virtual Academy for Food Security and Rural Prosperity, a new initiative of the MSSRF for ending hunger and eradicating rural poverty in India.

To assess the impact and sustainability of programmes for the use of ICTs in rural areas of India. More specifically, the project aimed to:

- Develop a set of parameters to make a choice of access technology and technology for powering the access devices
- Organise workshops and other interactions such as on-site consultations with policy makers to sensitise them to critical issues in the use of ICTs to promote human development in rural areas
- Fully transfer ownership of the project-supported rural telecentres from the project to rural communities to be completed within the timeframe of the project
- Develop ICT-based applications for rural areas, especially community banking online and distance education, to assess their potential to contribute to the sustenance of a rural ICT programme
- Conduct research on formation of multi-sectoral partnerships (private-public/government-NGOs) with rural communities to form a sustainable model of ICTs for rural areas
- Exchange research results with telecentre programmes in different parts of the world, to arrive at a more comprehensive picture of impact assessment and sustainability issues and its possible internalisation in project implementation

The project was able to provide several types of ICTs and ICT-based services to 12 different villages in the Union Territory of Pondicherry, and furthermore critically consider the advantages and disadvantages of each of these technologies. The technologies provided and assessed include: VHF Duplex radios, spread spectrum technology, satellite based internet connectivity, public address systems, and a community newspaper. Surprisingly, the newspaper was especially successful in creating awareness of and interest in the community knowledge centres, and in providing a forum in which villagers could publish news and concerns related specifically to development issues within their own community. Within two days of the release of the newspaper's first issue, the programme received over 60 phone calls from villagers interested in their services.

The technology provided to these rural communities has directly saved lives. Residents of Nallavadu, Pondicherry, survived the recent tsunami that devastated the area thanks to technology that MSSRF established with support from the IDRC. When one of the village residents received a phone call warning her of the approaching tsunami, she and her neighbours were able to broadcast the news across the village using a loudspeaker system that had been installed by MSSRF to inform fishermen of the water conditions. The entire village, more than 3,500 individuals, were able to evacuate in time to survive the tsunami.

The project held several workshops aimed at promoting awareness of ICTs and their uses in development, and at gaining input from the communities and policy makers involved. The first such workshop was held in October 2003 and another one the following year. These Policy Makers Workshops resulted in the creation of a National Alliance entitled "Mission 2007: Every Village a Knowledge Centre." This movement involves members of the private sector, cooperatives, non-governmental organisations, research and development institutions, women's associations, mass media, and appropriate government agencies in the mission to establish a knowledge centre in each of India's 600,000 villages by the year 2007, the 60th anniversary of the nation's independence.

The programme has provided training to knowledge centre volunteers on basic computer applications and volunteers, in turn, have trained tens of thousands of their neighbours. In 2003 alone, over 10,000 individuals were trained on computers through village knowledge centers. Software has also been developed to train the villagers in micro-enterprise and to assist self-help groups in managing their funds. These tools, combined with training on non-technological skills such as making ornamental artefacts from shells, has helped fishing village members, especially women, to alleviate some of the economic hardship faced during the annual 45 day fishing ban.

Not only has the programme benefited the villages of the Union Territory of Pondicherry, but it has produced a great wealth of information that can be exchanged with other programmes with similar objectives. One of the programme's initiatives is the annual South-South Exchange Travelling Workshop on ICT-enabled development, bringing together participants from different countries of Africa and Asia. African participants in the workshop were inspired to initiate a few programmes in their own countries based on what they learned. *Impact of ICTs in Rural Areas* was also able to learn from suggestions made during the workshop, and has since formed women self help groups in Nallavadu, based on an observation by workshop participants regarding lack of female participation in local government.

8.1. ICT Education in Rural Areas

Resources for rural education in India are severely limited, and often not used efficiently. Experiments such as that in Madhya Pradesh, where local rural communities were empowered (through its Education Guarantee Scheme) to create and control their schools, illustrate the possibilities of moving towards more decentralised delivery of education, with greater efficiency through local monitoring. Other examples of successful reform include better monitoring and the use of teachers' aides. In such cases, ICTs have not necessarily played a role, though they might in the future be used to enhance communication and experience-sharing across localities.

ICTs can enhance the power of experiments such as the Madhya Pradesh case by allowing even greater decentralisation, through the use of rural ICT kiosk operators who can act as teachers for smaller educational modules. The role of ICT kiosks is complementary to that of conventional schooling, as well as acting as a substitute. Since there are rural deficits in all the key components of education—teachers, textbooks and interaction—digital material and ICT-based interactions can ameliorate some of these deficits. Even more importantly, the use of ICTs allows for interactive, visually appealing content that appears to greatly enhance student interest, learning and retention.

The economics of production of digital media and use of digital services, with very low marginal costs, allow significant scaling up. In countries like India, development of appropriate educational materials (which can involve high fixed costs) can also be achieved economically, if target markets are defined and created by overcoming the relatively high fixed costs of obtaining access to IT resources. This is what the kiosk model provides. Thus, the amount of content that can be delivered cheaply through CDs and the Internet dwarfs what is possible through the traditional textbook model.

Rural ICT kiosk operators can provide such educational services at low cost, as part of an overall array of services. In the case of experiments with local control of education, parents are able to provide teachers with incentives for actually showing up and teaching. In the ICT case, the kiosk operator has an incentive to deliver such services since they increase the operator's income. Clearly the scale and cost of educational services in one-computer kiosks limits their effectiveness in providing anything like general education. There is thus no presumption or expectation that the use of ICTs in kiosks can substitute for basic education.

Nevertheless, educational services through rural ICT kiosks can provide an important complement, and even a multiplier effect, for more traditional educational efforts. One area where ICT-kiosk based rural education may have a significant role to play is in adult education, ranging from basic literacy to very specific skills for those who have received a conventional school education. The Indian educational system has no institutional mechanisms for adult education, and the quality and scope of vocational or skill-based education are extremely poor.

ICT-based education cannot be sufficient for many vocational skills, where hands-on experience is essential, but it can provide training in simple "knowledge economy" tasks such as using spreadsheets for accounting, inventory management and other business processes. Since computer-based wordprocessing is largely replacing the use of typewriters, basic secretarial skills also require access to computing resources. In the case of basic literacy and numeracy for adults, ICT-based learning offers a flexible option with relative anonymity, and therefore without social stigma. In many ways, therefore, rural ICT-kiosks can fill significant gaps that exist in the educational infrastructure of developing countries to cover the needs of "nontraditional" students and skills.

Initiatives such as n-Logue have focused on developing local language content, including print, digital text and digital video, for various types of education, though most obvious being training in basic computer skills. In addition to specialised content, a major role played by such kiosks is in providing low-cost access to IT tools for students who do not have this access at home or in school. Even when computers are available in rural schools, their availability may be limited. Rural IT kiosks provide more flexibility in access. Students use these computers for typing reports and searching for information.

In an ideal world, government-funded schools would make these educational tools sufficiently available within their systems, but that does not happen due to constraints on funding and poor incentives for implementation within government bureaucracies. Even in cases such as Drishtee, where education services were not part of formal offerings, individual kiosk operators used the kiosks for offering basic IT education to children whose parents were interested and willing to pay even small fees. In such cases, the operators enhanced their incomes as well as improving their social standing in the community.

In the case of some initial TARAhaat centers, women operators used the availability of the space where the computers were located to offer completely non-IT-related education (typically vocational, such as cooking and sewing classes) to village girls. This gender aspect was also important in cases where teenage girls had dropped out of school due to family pressures and social norms (e.g., the high school being "too far away" from home) but were able to receive some instruction from female kiosk operators. In such cases, rural IT kiosks have the potential to supplement more traditional correspondence courses, which have often been the educational avenue used by girls under social constraint with respect to mobility outside the home.

TARAhaat have focused on education delivery, primarily to secondary students and young adults who are interested in enhancing their skills. This is quite different from providing more basic, informal education to younger children. Certification by some recognised authority becomes important. In the case of TARAhaat, an initial arrangement was made to provide certification from the office of the Deputy Commissioner. At the same time, the Punjab Technical University (PTU) was given permission by the state government to offer classes through such kiosks, and that alternative became a valuable source of revenue to the kiosk owners.

Unfortunately, TARAhaat's management viewed the PTU classes as competition, and as having a possible negative impact on the nascent TARAhaat "brand." There was some upheaval in the relationships with the initial kiosk operators, and an imposition of an exclusivity clause for TARAhaat franchisees. It is understandable that an educational content provider might seek to impose such restrictions to protect its reputation. However, in this particular case, the development of new content was slower than promised, and the kiosk operators had to struggle initially.

In any case, the TARAhaat experience illustrates the importance of identifying the manner in which educational services will fit into the existing system, which is relatively rigid and overly bureaucratic, but does provide some quality control mechanisms. It is a standard argument within the education bureaucracy in India that private education providers must be very tightly controlled and regulated, with respect to entry and scale; else they will cheat unsuspecting victims. This perspective is overly paternalistic, and appears to treat clients for educational services as incapable of making rational choices.

An alternative regulatory model would emphasise private certification, market-based reputation building, and government-supported information dissemination with respect to quality. With this kind of supportive institutional reform, more varied, flexible and small-scale educational programmes could be offered in rural areas through ICT-based methods. Enabling the private sector to do this at low cost can free up government resources for primary education and basic literacy, where the government role is essential. The kinds of programs referred to here are supplementary training programmes outside basic education, such as learning business and conversational English, or particular software applications. In this respect, rural India has been ill-served by the Indian educational system, which favours the traditional urban, English-educated middle class.

8.2. ICT's for Rural Livelihoods

Developing appropriate ICTs (i.e. a framework) for sustainable development and sustainable livelihoods is, therefore, essential at grassroots level (i.e. at society level). ICTs is, however, not a panacea for grassroots level development problems, but it has the potential and opportunities to help the rural poor to leapfrog some of the traditional barriers to development by: improving access to information, expanding their market base, enhancing employment opportunities and making government services work better. There is a 'need to bridge theory and reality (i.e. grassroots)'.

Rural India desires to take advantage of 'knowledge-intensive' techniques for sustainability of its Stakeholding: farm and non-farm linkages. Grassroots level Information access (Contents) and Grassroots level access to Information (Networking) are the two essential components for grassroots level development strategies through ICT. The Digital Initiatives such as AgRIS, DISNIC, eCooperative and CoopNET, Digital SME etc are essential to usher in 'digital inclusion' for fostering rural prosperity.

8.2.1. Agricultural Resources Information System (AgRIS)

Agricultural Resources Information System (AgRIS) is the Central Sector Scheme for strengthening / promoting Agricultural Information System in the Department of Agriculture and Cooperation (DAC) Ministry of Agriculture. This Project is based on the recommendation of the Report of the Core Group- V of the Standing Committee on Agriculture and Soils, National Natural Resources Management System (NNRMS) of the Planning Commission (March, 2000). During the Tenth Plan, the Department of Agriculture and Cooperation, in association with National Informatics Centre (NIC), has undertaken 'Proof–of-Concepts-Projects' in districts across the country, facilitating the followings:

- Initiate pilot projects on 'Agricultural Resources information System' (AgRIS) in districts in order to work out the cost and efficiency of this project and then expand to the entire country;
- Develop a comprehensive database on various parameters related to land use, inputs (seeds, fertiliser, agricultural technology, agricultural credit) use, and water use;

- Development of decision support systems (DSSs) packages for strengthening advisory services to farmers; and
- Capacity building through Human Resources Development.

Converting millions of poor farmers to the use of new technologies has been a colossal task. The implementation of 'Agricultural Resources Information System (AgRIS)' will facilitate development of typology specific agriculture development plan in the country. As "resources application and agronomic practices" are to match with soil attributes and crop requirements, the Agricultural Resources Information System (AgRIS) is a "way-forward" to improve agricultural productivity in rural areas, and a much "needed domestic strategy" for sustainable rural livelihoods. The AgRIS is a step towards establishing a location-specific e-Government model for the Poor.

8.2.2. DISNIC Programme

While, in principle, the Panchayati Raj Institutions (PRIs) can be the effective bodies for local level planning and implementation, they may not be so in practice because of a number of constraints: most of the PRI Members do not have the necessary background in planning and implementation of development programmes. The Gram Sabhas will have to play a leading role in identification of local needs, mobilisation of local resources including human resources, identification of target group beneficiaries and monitoring of implementation of local projects.

Grassroots level Information access (Contents) and Grassroots level access to Information (Networking) are the two essential components for grassroots level development strategies through ICT. A significant barrier to the adoption of the appropriate technologies for rural villages has been the absence of analytic tools (databases) that accurately compare the alternative options, both conventional and renewable. The National Commission on Farmers (NCF) has recommended the establishment of Rural Knowledge Centres (RKCs) all over the country using modern information and communication technology (ICT) under the Mission 2007 Programme.

In India, 'district' is the basic administrative unit at the sub-state level and also consistent with the decentralised planning process prevailing at the grass-root. With the establishment of NICNET in districts numbering about in 1985-87, National Informatics Centre (NIC) has launched its 'district information system (DISNIC)' in about 27 sectors viz., agriculture, animal husbandry, education, health, industries, rural development, micro-level planning, etc, as an informatics tool for development planning and responsive administration. Indian village is a cognizable unit located in a specific agro-ecological and sociological environment. Its potentials and constraints for development are well known.

A significant barrier to the adoption of the appropriate technologies for rural villages has been the absence of analytic tools (databases) that accurately compare the alternative options, both conventional and renewable.

The DISNIC-PLAN new initiative will support building up databases (spatial and non-spatial), decision support systems, and communication systems to facilitate: sustainability of resources, poverty alleviation, and empowerment of women, full employment, production systems planning, infrastructure planning, and habitat planning. Production potentials of a village through 'circular-flows' and "chain-effect" should be understood. The objective of this consultation is to arrive at "an Informatics Blueprint that covers Villages" for economic and social development; derivation of various development indicators which will act as pointers to understand the development potentials as well as constraints for sustainable development; use of data and sensitisation at the lower level spatial units; relevance of geospatial intelligence, research, education, training and extension for micro level planning; institutional linkages and plan of action for implementation, etc.

8.2.3. e-Cooperatives and CoopNet

This is an Internet Enterprise Development Programme for fostering agricultural and rural industries. Rural Connectivity is the lifeline of rural economy. There are about 5.5 Lakh cooperative societies with a membership of more than 236 Million and working capital of more than Rs. 3400 Billion. Cooperatives have made remarkable progress in agriculture, banking, credit, agro-processing, storage, marketing, dairy, fishing and housing. This network covers 100% villages and 85% of rural households, and occupies a key position in agricultural development with respect to resources use, inputs use, harvesting of water resources, marketing channels, storage facilities, distribution channels, value addition, market information, and a regular monitoring network system. Cooperatives are also engaged in economic activities like disbursement of credit, distribution of agricultural inputs (seeds, fertilisers, and agro-chemicals), and arranging for Sanitary and Phyto Sanitary (SPS) measures of farm produces.

To begin with, it is suggested to network about 146000 Primary Agriculture and Credit Cooperatives (PACS), 19 National Level Cooperative Federations, 367 State Level Cooperative Federations and 2890 District level Cooperative Federations. Networking of Cooperatives through state-of-the-art technology is essential, which will facilitate to get connected to a National Data Centre (24/7 Infrastructure) for achieving the followings, for which an initial investment of Rs. 2500 Crores is required:

- Build relationships and alliances faster
- Re-engineer and integrate their processes
- Develop more and better value-added products and services;
- Share knowledge and experiences
- Enhance innovation
- Promote Web-based business trading

8.2.4. AgGMARKNET

As a step towards to globalisation of agriculture, the Union Ministry of Agriculture has embarked upon an ICT project: NICNET based Agricultural Marketing Information System Network (AGMARKNET) in the country. This AGMARKNET project has already networked 735 Agricultural Produces Wholesale Markets (APWMs), during 2000-02 and embarked upon additional 2000 Markets during the Tenth Plan Period (2002-2007). As of 31 December 2005, 2500 APWMs have been brought under the AGMARKNET Programme, which has facilitated in developing the database on 300 commodities and about 2000 varieties. The Government initiative of the networking of agricultural produce markets (AGMARKNET) and the AGMARKNET Portal would facilitate the development of B2B and B2C e-Commerce Model in the Country. This project has the potential of expansion to about 7000 Wholesale Markets located through out the country and further to 35000 Rural Markets in India. This ICT Project is a 'farmer-centric' project to put the progressive farmers on 'global free trade zone on Internet'.

8.2.5. Digital SMEs

Small and Medium Enterprises (SMEs) have always been the engine of growth in developing as well as in transition economies. In India, SMEs are the second biggest employment generators after agriculture, providing jobs to over 9.2 million people, and accounts for 39 per cent of industrial production and 34 per cent of exports. It is estimated that there are around 350 Urban SME clusters and approximately 2000 Rural and Artisan based clusters (Rural SMEs) in India. This does not include the Small and Marginal Farmers (SMFs), who constitutes of about 67% of the farming community in India.

The process of globalisation has impacted SMEs much more than larger business enterprises, and there have been a lot of studies which show that SMEs are at crossroads. While developed countries have already taken a lead in this direction, developing countries have yet to fully exploit this system particularly to invigorate Small and Medium Enterprises. There is a need for serious global thinking on how to ensure greater stability of SMEs, how to provide greater social security for those working in this sector, and, at the same time, how to retain the dynamic force that drives this secto.

Areas of business that are targeted for improvement of SMEs are: User profiling, Supply Chain, Value Chain, Customer-Relation-Management (CRM), SME Networks, and Suppliers Cooperation. The challenge for entrepreneurs is to think about creating solutions for the twin engines of future growth – Rural India and SMEs. Cluster approach, Industrial Estates, Industrial Growth Centres, Export Processing Zones, Industrial Parks and Integrated Infrastructure Development Centres etc., have been the spatial policies for infrastructure development of SMEs.

Agricultural informatics and communication in India According to the National IT Task Force recommendation, "the Government shall take all necessary steps to boost IT for Agriculture and Integrated rural development". The Ministry of Agriculture and National Informatics Centre (NIC) emphasised informatics for Agricultural development in the National Conference on "Informatics for Sustainable Agricultural Development (ISDA), Many follow up actions (ICT projects: AGMARKNET, DACNET, etc) were taken up, to provide relevant agricultural information in rural areas, helping farmers to improve their labour productivity, increase their yields, and realise a better price for their produce.

India is expected to become a 'Knowledge Society' by 2008 and by which time, any farmer in a remote village can demand and get the information about landuse planning for cropping strategy for farmers fields based on integrated information on soil, water, weather, fertiliser and pest management models; source to get proper seeds or good quality nursery plants; prevailing prices of farm equipments, agricultural produce, products and series of such set of information, which can lead to high productivity and optimum cost benefit to the farmers. To achieve this, the following things should happen:

- An agriculture information centre in each village;
- Interactive exchange of information for planning and day-to-day operations by farmers;
- Availability of all the extension and advisory services on demand.

8.3. Rise of New E-learning Technologies

Technologies to enable e-learning have tremendous potential for India. However, the benefits of these technologies must be made available to the Rural masses of India, otherwise, they will only widen the Digital Divide. Various technologies have been used over the years to propagate Distance Learning including the Radio, TV and now the Internet. There are several problems which affect Rural India but amongst them, a major problem is that literacy amongst farmers and Rural folk of India is very low. Emerging technologies such as Natural Language Interfaces and the Next Generation Internet will enable several innovative applications in elearning and enable parallel learning by helping to break the cycle of literacy followed by computer literacy.

8.3.1. Next Generation Internet

The Internet has grown so fast and wide that there is tremendous clogging happening on the Net. This choking has actually restricted the usage of the Internet and has not permitted applications such as Virtual Reality to be made available for Distance Learning purposes. The Next Generation Internet hopes to rectify that by providing higher bandwidth and better quality audio and video to enable Multimedia as well as a high amount of interactivity which is so essential in learning. The main projects currently leading the initiatives are the University Corporation for Advanced Internet Development which is monitoring two projects - the INTERNET 2 and the Abilene Project; the United States Government led Next Generation Internet Project and the National Science Foundation vBNS Backbone project.

The Internet 2 project is a joint project of Industry, Academia and Government. The basic purpose of the Next Generation Internet is to increase bandwidth and quality of service so that a new generation of applications could be possible on the Net. Some of the major initiatives of the Internet 2 Project include improving the Quality of Service, Middleware Initiative, Distributed Storage Initiative and Digital Video Initiative.

Amongst new applications which can be enabled with the Internet 2 are applications in Teaching and Learning. Learning is extremely easy when it is in the form of Virtual Reality, Multimedia and Collaborative interactivity. The Internet in its current form is unable to handle such heavy loads to enable such high quality distance learning to the Rural masses. Furthermore, as more and more users get on the Net, clogging is happening and the Net is unable to provide the level of quality needed for high-end interactive e-learning applications.

Applications which can be enabled by this technology include Virtual Laboratories and Digital Libraries. An interesting application of the Next Generation Internet is the area of Digital Libraries. Very high bandwidth and improved quality of service will permit applications such as continuous digital video and audio to be used for a very wide range of Library applications. The Advanced Internet will also permit Multimedia interfaces to the user of the Library as well as real time Consultation with experts over video conference.

Computer companies like Sun Microsystems are collaborating with the Internet 2 project to create a testbed for higher education. As, of today, this is restricted to the USA, but it could be extended to remote parts of India as well in future. Through this Testbed, students will be able to find and communicate with experts and other interested students through instant messaging and video conferencing. The Advanced Internet will also facilitate the development of Multimedia courseware across various development platforms in a highly distributed environment.

The student based in Rural India will be able to access the best Libraries and Laboratories in the World. The Next Generation Internet will also permit Virtual Laboratories by which students using Laboratory instruments connected to the Advanced Internet will be able to conduct a Laboratory experiment remotely. Therefore, a student in a Village in India will be able to virtual access the best Laboratories in the world.

8.3.2. Natural Language Interfaces

Natural Language Technology is another area, which could be of great use in e-learning. The technology, though in a nascent stage today, has a tremendous potential for Rural India. There is already a lot of work going on in this technology in India - prominent among them being the projects at CDAC, NCST, and at IIT Madras, Kanpur, Bombay.

Natural Language Interfaces is a way by which humans can communicate with the machine in a language that is natural to them. The Interfaces to Natural Languages can be to various areas including Intelligent Tutoring systems and Virtual Reality systems. In an e-learning environment these technologies could be of great use to build various customised training applications for the Rural Indian.

Rural based NGO's which are working for Rural development in India could then build such training applications directly without needing to wait for the IT industry to develop applications for them. Natural Language Interfaces along with touchscreen technology and voice enabled inputs could be a way by which the National Literacy mission could be achieved through a process of parallel learning and the cycle of literacy followed by computer literacy and usage can be broken. In addition, automatic translation systems are available today on the Web, which enable automatic translation of messages and content from English into several International languages. Developments can be made by which our villagers will be able to access the Net in their own language and hence dependency on an English translator will be reduced.

The Ministry of Information Technology is already involved in several projects such as Bharat Bhasha Kosh, Web based learning system in Indian languages, Speech Synthesis system at CEERI Pilani and Multilingual dictionaries. IIT Madras have developed an Indian Language word processor which has been tested at an NGO in Madras. Similarly NCST'S MATRA project 's focus is on man-machine synergy.

Natural Language interfaces can be used as front ends to databases as well as with Speech based systems. Both these technologies have great potential for Rural India since especially speech based systems since E-learning can actually be voice enabled through this technology and the villager will be freed from his lack of literacy and therefore inability to communicate.

References

Nilay M.Yajnik, "The potential of the Advanced Internet Project for India", *proceedings of the Annual Conference of the Computer Society of India,* Chennai, India, September 2000.

Bajpai, Piyush and Mayank Singh, "The Death of Indian Languages on the Internet", *The Case of Hindi, background paper, Indicus Analytics,* New Delhi, 2005.

Bhatnagar, Subhash and Robert Schware, *Information and Communication Technology in Development: Cases from India,* New Delhi: Sage Publications, 2000.

Bresnahan, Timothy and Manuel Trajtenberg, "General Purpose Technologies: 'Engines of Growth'", *Journal of Econometrics,* 1995.

Caspary, Georg and David O'Connor, "Providing Low-Cost Information Technology Access to Rural Communities in Developing

Countries: What Works? What Pays?", OECD Development Centre, *Working Paper No. 229*, November, 2003.

Dossani, Rafiq, D.C. Mishra and Roma Jhaveri, "Enabling ICT for Rural India", *Project Report*, Stanford University and National Informatics Centre, India, 2005.

Eggleston, Karen, Robert T. Jensen, and Richard Zeckhauser, "Information and Communication Technologies, Markets, and Economic Development", in The *Global Information Technology Report 2001-2002 Readiness for the Networked World*, ed., Geoffrey Kirkman *et al*, Oxford: Oxford University Press, 2002.

Gill, Anita, "Interlinked Agrarian Credit Markets in a Developing Economy: A Case Study of Indian Punjab", *paper presented in the International Conference on Globalization and Development Organized* by The Development Studies Association, U.K., at University Of Strathclyde, Glasgow 10-12 September, 2003.

9

Community Participation in Rural Education

Education takes place not only in schools but also within families, communities, and society. Communities and society must support parents and families in the upbringing, socialising, and educating of their children. Schools are institutions that can prepare children to contribute to the betterment of the society in which they operate, by equipping them with skills important in society. Schools cannot and should not operate as separate entities within society.

Since each group plays a different role in contributing to children's education, there must be efforts to make a bridge between them in order to maximise the contributions. Education takes place most efficiently and effectively when these different groups of people collaborate. Accordingly, it is important to establish and continuously attempt to develop partnerships between schools, parents, and communities.

Many research studies have identified various ways of community participation in education, providing specific channels through which communities can be involved in children's education. There are various forms of community participation: (a) research and data collection; (b) dialogue with policymakers; (c) school management; (d) curriculum design; (e) development of learning materials; and (f) school construction.

Parent and community support is one of the key factors to determine school effectiveness in Sub-Saharan Africa. They identify five categories of parent and community support that are relevant to the region: (1) children come to school prepared to learn; (2) the community provides financial and material support to the school; (3) communication between the school, parents, and community is frequent; (4) the community has a meaningful role in school governance; and (5) community members and parents assist with instruction.

There are three models of education and community. The first one is traditional community-based education, in which communities provide new generations of young people with the education necessary for transmitting local norms and economic skills. In this model, education is deeply embedded in local social relations, and school and community are closely linked. The government, being of little use in meeting the specialised training needs of industrialised economies, plays a minor role, providing little basis for political integration at the national level. The second model is government-provided education, in which governments have assumed responsibility for providing and regulating education.

The content of education has been largely standardised within and across countries, and governments have diminished the role of the community. However, a lack of resources and management incapability have proven that governments cannot provide the community with adequate the educational delivery, fully-equipped school buildings, and a full range of grades, teachers and instructional materials. This triggers the emergence of the collaborative model, in which community plays a supportive role in government provision of education.

There are different ways to help children succeed in school and later life, and focuses on partnerships of schools, families, and communities that attempt to:

(a) improve school programmes and school climate;
(b) provide family services and support;
(c) increase parents' skills and leadership;
(d) connect families with others in the school and in the community; and
(e) help teachers with their work.

The following various types of involvement to explain how schools, families, and communities can work productively together:

(1) parenting—to help all families to establish home environments that support children's learning at schools;
(2) communicating—to design effective forms of school-to-home and home-to-school communication that enable parents to learn about school programmes and their children's progress in schools as well as teachers to learn about how children do at home;
(3) volunteering—to recruit and organise parent help and support;
(4) learning at home—to provide information and ideas to families about how to help students at home with homework and other curriculum-related activities, decisions, and planning;
(5) decision making—to include families in school decisions, to have parent leaders and representatives in school meetings; and
(6) collaborating with the community—to identify and integrate resources as well as services from the community in order to strengthen school programmes, family practices, and student learning.

9.1. Importance of Community Participation in Education

The goal of any kind of activity that attempts to involve community and families/parents in education is to improve the educational delivery so that more children learn better and are well prepared for the changing world. There are various reasons to support the idea that community participation contributes to achieving this goal.

9.1.1. Maximising Limited Resources

Most governments all over the world have been committed to delivering education for their children. Particularly after the World Conference on Education for All, assembled in Jomiten, Thailand in 1990, an increasing number of countries have attempted to reach the goal of providing education for all. However, governments have found themselves incompetent to do so because of lack of resources and capacities. Learning materials as well as human resources are limited everywhere, particularly in developing countries. The focus has shifted to finding efficient and effective ways to utilise existing limited resources.

Although some communities have historically been involved in their children's education, it hasn't been fully recognised that communities themselves have resources to contribute to education, and they can be resources by providing local knowledge for their children. Involving parents, families, and communities in the process of research and data collection can reveal to them factors that contribute to lower enrolment and attendance, and poor academic performance in their schools. Furthermore, parents are usually concerned about their children's education, and often are willing to provide assistance that can improve the educational delivery. In places where teacher absenteeism and poor performance are critical issues, parents can be part of the system of monitoring and supervising teachers, ensuring that teachers arrive at classrooms on time and perform effectively in the classrooms. Parents and communities are powerful resources to be utilised not only in contributing to the improvement of educational delivery but also in becoming the core agent of the education delivery .

9.1.2. Relevant Curriculum and Learning Materials

Communities' and parents' involvement helps achieve curriculums and learning materials that reflect children's everyday lives in society. When children use textbooks and other materials that illustrate their own lives in their community, they can easily associate what they are learning with what they have already known.

In Papua New Guinea, community schools set the goal to link the culture of the pupils' home community with the culture of the school. Accordingly, the schools consider the community as the center of learning as well as the focus of education. As a result, the community schools have become central to the national curriculum development which enables community life, such as festivals, customs, musical instruments, and local business activities, to be reflected in the curriculum.

In each learning task, self instructional textbooks guide students to identify examples and cultural elements from their own experience and allows local materials to be accumulated in the learning centers. The oral tradition is transcribed and classified. Local crafts, jobs and economic activities, health problems, geography, landscapes, transport, sports, dances, food, animals, vegetation, and minerals are also described and classified for use in learning experiences.

9.1.3. Identifying and Addressing Problems

Communities can help identify and address factors that contribute to educational problems, such as low participation and poor academic performance. This is well illustrated in the case of the Gambia, in which the techniques of Participatory Rural Appraisal (PRA) were adapted to education. The work was carried out in order to understand why girls do not attend schools, to mobilise communities around these problems, and to assist them in organising their own solutions. Thirteen local researchers were trained in PRA which allowed the participation of all groups in a community, including illiterate and literate, young and old, females and males. A sample of seven rural villages was selected, in which a team of researchers worked with residents focusing on group discussions, mapping of the village, calendars of income and expenditure, and matrices of community and education problems.

The research revealed that key disincentives to educating girls were related to: (a) inadequate supply of schools, particularly middle schools; (b) high costs of schooling; (c) higher risk of early pregnancy; (d) loss of respect for traditional values, particularly obedience and humility towards husbands; and (e) perceptions, particularly among men, that girls will be less successful in life generally. A further step was taken in two of the seven communities where residents were invited to select six important problems from a longer list that they had developed previously which they could begin to address in a practical way, utilising mainly their own resources. Various options for solving problems were devised and those seeming to have the highest chance of success were integrated into a Community Action Plan.

9.1.4. Promoting Girls' Education

Community participation can contribute to promoting girls' education. Through participating in school activities and frequently communicating with teachers, parents and communities can learn that girls' education contributes to the improvement of various aspects of their lives, such as increased economic productivity, improved family health and nutrition, reduced fertility rates, and reduced child mortality rates. Involving parents and communities in discussions as part of school activities also helps to identify factors that prevent girls from schooling.

Parents are encouraged to express their concern, and reasons why they are not sending their daughters to school. For instance, many parents in rural areas are reluctant to send their daughters to schools located in distance, concerned about the security of their daughters on the way to and from the school. In addition, since girls are important labours in the household, helping their mothers to do the chores and take care of their young siblings. The time that requires going to and from school seems too much to waste for the parents. These issues are serious obstacles and have to be addressed and overcome in order to promote girls' education.

Involving parents and communities in school activities also helps to identify possible teachers in the community, especially local female teachers which greatly help girls' education. Furthermore, in places where communities are indifferent in girls' education, elderly people or religious leaders who are respected by community members can convince them to send their girls to schools, if the dialogue with these respected people takes place successfully.

9.2. Creating and Nourishing Community-School Partnerships

There are various ways to bring parents and community members closer to schools which they serve, including:

(a) minimising discontinuities between schools and communities, and between schools and families;

(b) minimising conflicts between schools and communities, schools and families, teachers and parents, and what is taught in school and what is taught at home;

(c) making easy transition of pupils going from home to school;

(d) preparing pupils to engage in learning experiences; and

(e) minimising cultural shock of new entrants to schooling.

Communities can contribute to schools by sending respected community members, such as religious leaders or tribe heads, to the classrooms and talk about community history, traditions, customs, and culture, which have been historically celebrated in the community. Schools themselves can contribute to community efforts by developing sustainable solutions to local problems.

One example is found in the Social Forestry, Education and Participation pilot project (SFEP) in Thailand. The purpose of the project is to change teaching, learning, and school-community relations by involving fifth and six grade students in studies of local village problems related to forest management. The students visited communities and asked questions about village history and the origins and causes of various forest-related problems. Community members helped them understand concepts taught in schools, and students used any resource available within the communities to enhance their understanding. In addition to gathering data from villagers, students went to nearby forests to study plants and animals as part of their regular science lessons. Some local villagers came along as "experts" to help them understand various species indigenous to that village.

9.2.1. Realising Democracy

Where schools are perceived as authoritarian institutions, parents and community members do not feel welcomed to participate in their children's education. They are not capable of taking any responsibility in school issues and tend to feel that education is something that should be taken care of by educational professionals at schools many people, especially minority groups in many developing countries, develop this kind of negative attitudes towards schools because they are not treated by teachers with respect. For instance, those who do not speak the country's official language and embrace other than mainstream traditions and culture feel discouraged in classrooms where teachers don't show respect to their linguistic and cultural diversity.

In the history, there were times when children were prohibited from speaking their first language in schools and they got severe punishment when they broke the rule imposed by the school or the government. This educational environment is unfavourable to parents and children and, therefore, contributes to these students' low participation, poor academic performance, and high repeat and dropout rates. Involving communities in schools is a way of reaching democracy through identifying and addressing inequities embedded in institutions and society as a whole. In addition, it is a strategy to create an environment in which parents feel comfortable participating in schools.

Moreover, parental involvement in education is seen as a right, or as an outright democratic value in some countries. According to OECD study, "in Denmark, England, and Wales, parents have a right to be represented on the governing bodies of schools; in France, they have a right to representation on a whole range of policy-making bodies; the Parent's Charter gives English and Welsh parents a number of rights, including the right to certain information from the school; in Spain, the Constitution recognises the right of teachers, parents and students to participate in defining the scope and nature of the education service; and forthcoming legislation in Ireland will place parents at the center of the education process, and give them a wide range of statutory rights in relation to education."

9.2.2. Increasing Accountability

Parental involvement in education, particularly in school governance, is seen as a means of making schools more accountable to the society which funds them. This has been witnessed in some places such as England and Wales, Canada and the United States. The notion of parental involvement for accountability derives from a more market-oriented concept in which school-family partnerships are viewed rather like business partnership, through which the two parties receive mutual and complementary benefits which enable them to operate more effectively.

The accountability is developed through routine parents' meetings and reporting systems on student progress. When parents contribute their time, labour, materials, land, and funds, they tend to be more involved in school activities, including participating in meetings with teachers and monitoring teachers' performance. Teachers and school staff, in turn, feel more obliged to deliver better education for the students in order to respond to the needs of parents and communities. Participation can greatly help develop accountability, which contributes to improving the education delivery.

A Community Support Programme (CSP) process in Balochistan, Pakistan, was developed to ensure village commitment to girls' education. It defines the responsibilities of the community and the Directorate of Primary Education. The greater the participation of the community, both financially and in-kind, means they are more likely to demand accountability from staff. Parents are also more involved in the day-to-day management of the school where they see what is happening and what needs to be corrected. The CSP has formed Village Education Committee (VEC) that consists of five to seven men whose daughters will attend the school. VECs are formed to serve as the school's official representative to the government. The forming of VECs has contributed to the CSP's establishment of an organisational structure that encourages teachers' and local administrators' accountability to parents. Once the school is opened, VEC members are empowered to report teacher attendance or behaviour problems to the government and to recommend teachers for training.

9.2.3. Ensuring Sustainability

One of the major factors to ensure sustainability of programmes is the availability of funds, whether from governments, private institutions, or donor organisations. In this regard, community participation in education cannot ensure the sustainability of schools by itself since communities oftentimes have to rely on external funding to keep the programme sustained. However, involving community is a way to ensure that the benefits brought by a development programme will be maintained after the external interventions are stopped. Thus, sustainability is dependent on the degree of self-reliance developed in target communities and on the social and political commitment in the wider society to development programmes that support the continuation of newly self-reliance communities. Community members are expected to be actively involved in the process of interventions through planning, implementation, and evaluation.

Furthermore, they are expected to acquire skills and knowledge that will later enable them to take over the project or programme.

9.2.4. Improving Home Environment

Community participation can contribute to preparing and improving home environment, by encouraging parents to understand about the benefits of their children's schooling. A World Bank study which analysed primary education in India, discovered that families aware of the importance of education can contribute much to their children's learning achievement, even in disadvantaged districts. It also shows that students from families that encouraged children's schooling, by allocating time at home for study, encouraging reading, and supporting their children's educational aspirations, scored significantly higher on tests of learning achievement. Furthermore, families who are involved in schools not only have a better understanding about education but also become more willing to cooperate with schools in attempts to improve children's learning. In addition, parents can help their children with homework, and make sure that children are physically ready to learn at schools.

9.2.5. Improving Education

Community participation can contribute to education delivery through various channels. The following is a list of ways through which communities can contribute to the education delivery:

- advocating enrolment and education benefits;
- boosting morale of school staff;
- raising money for schools;
- ensuring students' regular attendance and completion;
- constructing, repairing, and improving school facilities;
- contributing in labour, materials, land, and funds;
- recruiting and supporting teachers;
- making decisions about school locations and schedules;
- monitoring and following up on teacher attendance and performance;
- forming village education committees to manage schools;

- actively attending school meetings to learn about children's learning progress and classroom behaviour;
- providing skill instruction and local culture information;
- helping children with studying;
- garnering more resources from and solving problems through the education bureaucracy;
- advocating and promoting girls' education;
- providing security for teachers by preparing adequate housing for them;
- scheduling school calendars;
- handling the budget to operate schools;
- identifying factors contributing to educational problems (low enrolment, and high repetition and dropout); and
- preparing children's readiness for schooling by providing them with adequate nutrition and stimuli for their cognitive development.

Among various forms of community contributions, some are specifically aimed to support teachers. For instance, communities can provide, or construct, housing for teachers who are from outside of the community. In rural areas, lack of qualified teachers is critical, and preparing a safe environment and housing is necessary to attract teachers, particularly female teachers, who otherwise tend to stay in or go to urban areas.

Teachers can benefit from communities' active participation in their children's schools. For example, community members themselves can be a rich resource to support teachers' practice in classrooms by facilitating children's learning. In the Social Forestry, Education and Participation pilot project (SFEP) in Thailand, local villagers came to schools and helped students understand various species indigenous to that village. Community members can help students understand concepts which teachers teach in classrooms by having the students coming into community, interacting with community members who are knowledgeable about village history and the certain issues faced by the community. Respected community members can become knowledgeable lectures who can come to the classrooms, and teach students issues faced by the community.

Also, community members can support teachers by contributing their skill to speak the local language when the majority of students don't understand the teacher's language of instruction. They can attend classrooms as interpreters who not only translate languages but also help teachers as well as students by bridging the gap that exists between cultural values of teachers and those of students. Furthermore, parents and community members can contribute to teachers' teaching materials by providing them with knowledge and materials that are locally sensitive and more familiar to children.

Community participation in education can also be a powerful incentive for teachers. Teachers' absenteeism, and lack of punctuality to show up in classrooms on time are serious problems in many places. Among many other reasons, lack of monitoring system is one of the critical factors contributing to these problems. When teachers are monitored and supervised for their attendance and performance by communities, they tend to be more aware of what they do. Feedback from parents and the community about their teaching performance can be a strong tool to motivate teachers, if schools are also collaborative.

9.3. Challenges

Involving communities in the education delivery requires facing and tackling a number of challenges. Challenges vary from one stakeholder to another because each group has its own vision to achieve the common goal of increasing educational access and improving its quality. The following section attempts to turn to specific challenges and problems that have been witnessed among teachers, and parents and communities.

9.3.1. Teachers

Not all teachers welcome parents' and communities' participation in education. They tend to feel that they are losing authority within schools, as power is taken by community and parents. At the same time, they are encouraged to involve community members who sometimes are not willing to get involved in any school activities.

The complex relationship between teachers and parents focus on the decentralisation of education. Many parents in many countries would like to be more involved in selecting and monitoring teachers. For example, the impacts of the El Salvador's EDUCO project in which parents are responsible for school management and monitor teachers, the teachers feel threatened by parental involvement, believing that it will diminish public regard for their professional status.

9.3.2. Parents and Communities

Not all parents and community members are willing to get involved in school activities. Some have had negative schooling experiences themselves, some are illiterate and don't feel comfortable talking to teachers, and getting involved in any kind of school activities. They feel they don't have control over the school. Some parents and families are not willing to collaborate with schools because they cannot afford to lose their economical labour by sending their children. Even though they see the benefits to send children to schools, opportunity costs are oftentimes too high to pay.

A World Bank study of social assessment on EDUCO, community managed-schools, in El Salvador reveals that even though the parents valued education and had a positive attitude regarding the teachers, they were suspicious about the government. This wariness, combined with lack of communication, fostered the fear that education would be privatised and parents would have to pay for education services. Parents are optimistic about the economic value of education, but their optimism decreases when they are asked to think about the role of education in their own lives. Furthermore, because of parents' relative lack of education and the way the traditional school systems are structured, parents and teachers perceive their roles as separate from one another, without substantial parental interaction with teachers or involvement in the schools themselves.

References

Bray, Mark, *Decentralisation of Education: Community Financing*, Washington, DC: World Bank, 1996.

Campfens, Hubert. (Ed.), *Community Development around the World: Practice, Theory, Research, Training*, Toronto, Buffalo, and London: University of Toronto Press, 1997.

Colletta, Nat J. and Gillian Perkins, "Participation in Education", *Environment Department Papers, Paper No.001. Participation Series,* Washington, DC: The World Bank, 1995.

Epstein, Joyce Levy, "School/Family/Community Partnerships: Caring for the Children We Share", In Phi Delta Kappan. v.76, May 1995.

Epstein, Joyce L.; Lucretia Coates; Karen Clark Salinas; Mavis G. Sanders; and Beth S. Simon, "School, Family, and Community Partnerships: Your Handbook for Action", 1997.

Gaynor, Cathy, *Decentralisation of Education: Teacher Management,* Washington, DC: World Bank, 1998.

Goldring, E. B., "Community and Parents' Participation in Curriculum Decisions", In *The International Encyclopedia of Education,* Second Edition Volume 2, 1994.

Heneveld, Ward and Helen Craig, "Schools Count: World Bank Project Designs and the Quality of Primary Education in Sub-Saharan Africa", Washington, DC: The World Bank, 1996.

Lovell, Catherine H., *Breaking the Cycle of Poverty: The BRAC Strategy,* West Hartford, Connecticut: Kumarian Press, Inc., 1992.

Narayan-Parker, Deepa, *Designing community based development,* Washington, DC: The World Bank, 1995.

OECD (Organisation for Economic Co-operation and Development), *Parents as Partners in Schooling,* Paris: OECD, Center for Educational Research and Innovation, 1997.

Rugh, Andrea and Heather Bossert, "Involving Communities: Participation in the Delivery of Education Programmes", *Submitted to Advancing Basic Education and Literacy Project,* Washington, DC: Creative Associates International, Inc., 1998.

Shaeffer, Sheldon (Ed.), "Collaborating for Educational Change: the Role of Teachers, Parents and the Community in School Improvement", Paris: UNESCO, International Institute for Educational Planning, 1992.

Williams, James H., "The Role of the Community in Education", In *The Forum For Advancing Basic Education and Literacy,* Volume 3, Issue 4, September 1994.

World Bank, "Pakistan, Improving Basic Education: Community Participation, System Accountability, and Efficiency", *Sector Report No. 14960-PAK,* Washington, DC: World Bank, Population and Human Resources Division, Country Department I, South Asia Region, 1996.

10

Knowledge-sharing for Rural Community Development

Each society has generated their own means of transmitting knowledge from generation to generation, and while some knowledge has always been held in reserve by certain crafts or occupations, the great majority of knowledge has been shared freely. This experimentation and exchange are precisely what have enabled improvements in species and techniques, adapting crops to local conditions. In addition, it has contributed to the conservation of biological diversity, ensuring that the ecosystem remains robust. In this way, although people have not been altogether immune from disasters and plagues, they have been equipped with mechanisms to overcome them.

10.1. Towards a Transformative Knowledge

Knowledge necessarily implies a process of assimilation and transformation by the human mind. A data base can contain information—that is, organised data—but for this data to become knowledge, it must be appropriated and confronted by reality. For scientist Albert Einstein, the only source of knowledge is experience.

The popular education theorist, Paulo Freire, considers that to know is to construct categories of thought with which one can appraise the world, making its interpretation and transformation possible. In addition, he recognises that generating knowledge is a social process: There is no knowledge in existence that has not been born out of preexisting knowledge and that which exists today came from that which existed before. For this reason, to share knowledge is a condition for its creation. In a given society, the choice of which knowledge is developed is not a neutral process. Currently, what is considered "universal knowledge" is increasingly that which is developed to serve powerful economic interests. So much so that in the last quarter century, publicly-financed research has been drastically reduced, giving way to that financed by large corporations.

The World Bank—an institution which also boasts of being a knowledge bank—expressed this vision of "universal knowledge" in a document which argues how knowledge management can favor development:

> Developing countries need not reinvent the wheel (...) Rather than re-create existing knowledge, poorer countries have the option of acquiring and adapting much knowledge already available in the richer countries. With communication costs plummeting, transferring knowledge is cheaper than ever."

Among the national strategies to reduce inequalities, the Bank mentions three means of facilitating this acquisition: "an open trading regime, foreign investment, and technology licensing"; in addition, it proposes corporatising research institutes.

10.2. Privatisation of Knowledge

In this dichotomy concerning visions, the privatisation of knowledge (via the ever greater expansion of intellectual property rights) and its nature as a public good comes into play. From their original purpose of stimulating creativity, while assuring reasonable remuneration to authors and inventors, copyright and patents are expanding today into more and more areas—including forms of life, such as genetically-modified seeds and genomes.

One of the areas in which the impact of such policies is felt most intensely is in the countryside. Without giving them recognition, transnational companies are patenting the ancestral knowledge of indigenous peoples, and then trying to earn royalties from these same rural populations for using the seeds that they have patented. In the face of this problem, Latin American countries have been slow to react to ensure adequate protection of the traditional knowledge of their peoples.

In fact, the production and exchange of knowledge and information has a peculiarity that distinguishes it from material goods. Through the process of sharing, knowledge is not lost, rather it is multiplied and enriched. In other words, intellectual common goods can be used concurrently by a countless number of people, without interfering with or destroying the shared resource. For this reason, the economy of symbolic goods does not correspond to the same parameters as that of material goods.

With the growth of digitisation and the Internet, the cost of reproducing and distributing symbolic goods (texts, data, audio-visuals, computer software, music, etc.) is close to zero; but as these products are very easy to copy for free, this is seen as a threat by those who are trying to profit from them. This leads to demands for establishing and extending intellectual property rights and further restricting copyright. In the majority of cases, the main beneficiaries of such rights are no longer the individual authors and inventors, but rather large corporations. One of the consequences of this push toward privatisation of knowledge is that it jeopardises the principle of international law, recognising cultural and scientific creation as the common property of humanity and as a source for new creations.

"Collective intelligence" initiatives stand out among the citizen-based responses to this phenomenon, one of the main expressions of which is the free software movement. This movement defends four freedoms: the freedom to use computer software; the freedom to study and adapt programmes; the freedom to distribute copies, as well as to upgrade and share programmes so that everyone benefits. These liberties are similar to those claimed by the movement for the free exchange and improvement of seeds.

10.3. Potential of Information and Communication Technologies

The issue of knowledge for rural development, formulated within the field of international development, in the last decade, great expectations have arisen from the potential of new information and communication technologies (ICTs). Dominant discourse focuses on the need to overcome the "digital divide," pointing out that the lack of access to these technologies will only deepen gaps in development, whereas greater access would allow rural communities to connect with information and knowledge that will supposedly help them to overcome underdevelopment. These arguments have led to considering programmes which give marginalised populations access to technology as a solution for underdevelopment.

Undoubtedly, access to telecommunications should be guaranteed as a universal service. However, there is no evidence to demonstrate that these technologies can, in and of themselves, provide solutions to the problems of rural development indicated above. In practice, many projects based on a technological approach have failed, when they start from the view that technology is a tool with which to channel knowledge from the outside, without regard for the existing knowledge system within the community concerned, their values or their culture. Nonetheless, there is mounting evidence, that through a process of community appropriation, these technologies can indeed be a strategic component of more integrated solutions.

Various initiatives that have started from a process of the communities themselves identifying their needs and priorities, have taken on a search for methods and methodologies, in which ICTs are identified as one of many possible options which may be harnessed for development and exchange of knowledge. There are no universal prescriptions to achieve this, but some common criteria can be identified. The sharing of experiences, including the successes and errors encountered, can help optimise integration of these tools.

10.4. Media and Knowledge Sharing

10.4.1. Documenting and Recording

Documenting and recording the outcomes of activities and projects makes extensive use of different media instruments, in workshops and exchange activities. The objective of documentation is to capture the experiences, ideas and collective creations developed during the activity in order to copy, archive or refer back to them. In knowledge sharing processes, documentation is essential to creating an explicit archive of what was collectively created, for which photos, videos, presentations, transcripts and documents used during the activity are very important.

These materials and media together tell the story of what took place. They compile the information shared or created during the workshop and, using visual, audiovisual or digital means, they ensure that people can remember what took place and communicate this to others who were absent. A wide variety of resources, with different qualities, can be used to document and record processes and activities. Organisations have the most experience using media in this way. Some have also been quite innovative and have created interactive presentations about what was shared.

10.4.2. Methodological Support

The potential for digital media or multimedia to be integrated into knowledge sharing methodology and to help create sharing conditions has not been well-explored. One example of such an application would be if part of the workshop interaction takes place in a web forum and the forum is made part of the methodology. Instead of being a side process, the forum could become a subgroup for participants who are geographically distant. The web forum could also be used as a storage facility that is progressively filled with ideas, links, examples and resources used during the workshop. We've also used video. Using video in place of a live expert presentation has given us very positive results when it has been integrated into our methodology and used for a specific purpose. For example it can pose questions for debate or provided a starting point for discussion amongst the group leading towards a common creation.

Video can also be useful to help explain a complicated topic for participants to use when they return to their organisations. Videos, however, require a greater effort to produce than most other materials and are also expensive. As a result, their use must be clearly justified and it must be well integrated into the methodology. The quality of editing and images, its availability in multiple languages (with subtitles or translation), and the documents or digital files that accompany the video, are all factors that may hinder or enhance its usefulness to present a subject and generate discussion.

Each methodological design includes an outline of the required materials which will help to advance the process rather than being mere decorations. For example, different colored ribbons can be used to help identify groups, cardboard cards can be put together to create a mural of everyone's ideas, a giant map can help participants to collectively identify where they're from.

10.4.3. Creating and Transforming Media

Another aspect of media that we've wanted to build into knowledge sharing experiences, as far as possible, is to integrate training for participants so that they can transform both the content they create as well as the media they use during the interaction. The idea is that participants manipulate and transform media by determining its role in the knowledge sharing process, the way it will be applied and what kind of results will be produced. In this way, media becomes an essential part of the sharing process and enhances collective creation.

There are a series of relationships affecting the interweaving of multimedia with knowledge sharing process.

- *Individual participants representing a group*: workshop participants usually represent a larger group that may be located in another part of the country, of the region or the world. In knowledge sharing methodologies, as well as in the use of media, we try to balance the individual participant's inputs with the inputs from the network or group that he or she represents. Media can help to illustrate this relationship in which participants are representing others. Internet tools for collective creation such as blogs, wikis, forums and chats are useful in this regard.
- *Adapting audiovisual and symbolic language to the local context*: we try to ensure that symbols, images and language used in our materials are relevant to the groups involved considering their culture and context. References perceived to be foreign or irrelevant may hinder the sharing process, which also happens frequently when people encounter new or unknown technologies. Sometimes the simplest media is the most useful in helping participants to develop their own language in order to share and defend their ideas.
- *Relationship between media and the objectives*: it is necessary to strike a balance between the space we give to the media

we have prepared for a process and how the process is evolving toward the desired objectives. Often some of the materials we prepare for a workshop are left unused because dynamics within the workshop change, making them irrelevant or inappropriate. Media must always have a purpose that is directly related to the goals. Materials cannot be merely decorative; they need to be well-considered and suitable.

– *Participant as producer*: In order to appropriate the process, participants must see themselves and their ideas reflected in the media used. Materials that are too elaborate and which don't allow for changes or intervention by participants may be perceived as foreign or difficult to relate to. We try to use media that are simple, interchangeable, easy to reproduce and multi-purpose. As a result, participants can decide what form they will take and which ideas they will represent.
– *"Live" media production*: We have had various experiences and different results in on-the-spot media production. While it's easier to prepare a video or set of photographs in advance, live production is a much more valuable experience. However, technical difficulties, lack of resources and the pace of live production may affect the quality of the final outcome.

10.5. Community Development Process

The Community Information Resource Centre (CIRC) is an integral part of the development struggle in the community. One of the challenges it faces is how to encourage and support the processing of knowledge by community members, so they may find solutions to the community's problems. The community development process itself creates a large part of the information content needed by the community. Problem identification and learning (knowledge processing) are linked. Together they make up one process. This process is most effective, if it is a group effort rather than an individual undertaking. For example, some community members may discuss HIV/AIDS and how it is affecting everyone in their community. The discussion may raise the challenges of getting more accurate information about this disease and how it spreads, in order to counter rumours and superstitious explanations. After the information is gathered from different sources and shared by the group, the next step may include a programme of activities to fight against the spread of HIV/AIDS in the community.

The CIRC will be made up of information content coming from two sources: internal sources within the community and external sources, such as books, newspapers, audio-visual materials, the Internet, and the advice of health and extension workers.

10.5.1. Internal Information and Knowledge Sources

In building information content, it is important to start with the information and knowledge that exist in the community itself. The internal information and knowledge content comes from two sources: namely, indigenous knowledge, and locally created information.

10.5.1.1. Indigenous Knowledge

Knowledge is a product of human thought, action and experience. Each culture contains a knowledge base from which its members receive understanding and an interpretation of the world. Indigenous knowledge is rich in cultural knowledge that provides identity to young people. Indigenous knowledge forms part of the community's information and knowledge resources. In most communities, this knowledge has difficulty surviving. Difficulties arise because traditions and cultures are often the object of massive attacks and questions by the dominant culture. The group with power casts aside and disorganises the knowledge and traditions that rural groups and groups without power use to define themselves and their view of the world.

In decreasing the value of indigenous and local knowledge resources, the channels of traditional knowledge communication have been cut off. The younger generation has been de-linked from their own culture and traditions. This separation makes it difficult for the older generation to transfer this rich cultural heritage to the next generation. Young people, in turn, are estranged. They develop anti-social behaviours to attract attention and sympathy.

In the past, Western knowledge, with its powerful tools, was thought to have all the answers to humanity's problems. However, it has become clear that the industrialised countries have, for example, mismanaged the physical environment. They have discovered technologies that are very destructive to human life. They have failed to discover cures to some of the worst diseases of our century. These failures have forced scientists to recognise the value of the knowledge that is part of indigenous and traditional cultures. Some of the reasons for the destruction of the indigenous knowledge base include:

a) Young people turning away from their elders and breaking an ancient chain of orally communicated knowledge;
b) An education system which is de-linked from the indigenous knowledge base and aimed at proving that external information is better than indigenous knowledge;
c) The destruction of the homes of indigenous populations by urbanisation, farming and commercial activities, such as logging and mining;
d) Propaganda from the "modernisation-oriented" mass media and political elite that traditional ways of doing things are never as good as external ways of doing things and should be rejected.

The production of knowledge is a natural human process. Ongoing production of knowledge is a critical element in the use of information and knowledge. However, if there is an attempt to prevent or destroy the growth of new indigenous knowledge, some parts of the knowledge base may become outdated or may die through lack of fresh input. One of the key roles of the CIRC is to gather, preserve, and make available indigenous knowledge. This knowledge should be evaluated in the same way as external knowledge coming into the community. At the local level, vast quantities of knowledge exist, locked away in the collective memory of people as inherited knowledge and personal experience. These stories should be evaluated carefully and recorded so that they can be put to use.

The task of reviving indigenous knowledge should go hand in hand with identifying negative traditional practices which make it difficult to achieve development for all groups in society.

The negative traditional practices should be changed through public discussions and campaigns. Such practices may include, for example: Female Genital Mutilation (FGM), discrimination against women, abduction of women, discrimination or violence against other ethnic groups or tribes because of historical enmities, glorification of war with neighbouring tribes, violence against women, ill-treatment of people with disabilities. To address negative practices, the best approach is to create a committee which will list them and decide how to remove them from society.

10.5.1.2. External Information and Knowledge Content

External information and knowledge sources are also vital because some human development problems are similar worldwide. By gaining access to information and knowledge sources that bring this experience to the community, members save valuable time and resources. They are able to learn and adapt good ideas from grassroots communities in other countries. One barrier to accessing information from external sources is language. This barrier shows itself in various ways:

a) Many printed materials are written by the elite for other elites, and are often unreadable by an ordinary person.

b) Sometimes the materials are written in difficult language. An ordinary person looking for practical information cannot understand how to apply the information. In such a case, the document is available, but inaccessible at the same time.

c) Most local languages have few written materials. It is, therefore, recommended that the CIRC identify useful materials that outline the experiences of other grassroots communities in the world. These can be translated directly to the local language, in order to make their valuable experience accessible to the community.

Despite the problems noted above, information, in the form of publications, audio-visual materials and the Internet, may bring ideas from outside the community. Sources include materials from:

a) *Government agencies*: Information comes from ministries and different governmental agencies, working in areas, such as agriculture and livestock, health and social services, education and adult education, and science and technology. In many countries, ministries of agriculture and health produce magazines, pamphlets, and posters. They also often have well-developed collections of video materials to support extension services.

b) *Educational institutions*: Educational institutions include universities, adult education institutes, and research centres.

c) *Development organisations (both national and international)*: These include non-governmental organisations (NGOs) and voluntary agencies.

d) *United Nations (UN) agencies*: These agencies, such as the Food and Agriculture Organisation (FAO), the World Health Organisation (WHO), the United Nations Development Programme (UNDP), the United Nations High Commissioner for Refugees (UNHCR) , and the United Nations Children's Fund (UNICEF) provide lots of development information in printed, electronic and audio-visual format.

e) *Donor communities*: These include the European Union (EU) and Embassy Development Agencies (Sweden, German, Canada, Finland, Norway, Denmark, The Netherlands, Japan and others).

f) *Networking*: In addition to getting information packages, some of the above organisations are also quite useful in suggesting and supporting partnerships and communication among persons and groups involved in similar projects throughout the world. Such information networks are important both as a source of information and also as a means of exchanging ideas and sharing experiences.

10.6. Information Sharing and Processing in the Community

The Community Information Resource Centre (CIRC) model is that of an agency, actively involved in development goals. It serves as an information focal point for local projects, across a whole range of community development activities. Unlike many public libraries, the CIRC is not primarily a provider of external information sources to passive consumers. The starting point of a good programme for information communication, processing and sharing in the community is an accurate idea of the information seeking patterns of community members. It is important to understand the use of information by different groups in the community. Such a base will ensure that every group has access, at the very least, to the basic minimum information it needs.

10.6.1. Information Seeking Patterns

The information seeking patterns of various groups in society differ. Information centre workers must be aware of these differences and why they exist, in order to support access to information for the whole community. Each of the groups needs slightly different communication strategies. The main groups that need special attention are:

10.6.1.1. Semi-literate and New Literate Community Members

Communicating adequate information to this group is essential because they may constitute 30% or more of all the adult population. These members have a big contribution to make in the development process of the community. At present, most of the information flow reaching them works through the oral information system. Some of the elders in this group will be "experts" and rich sources of indigenous knowledge. It is very important not to regard the oral information system as separate or opposed to the print-based information system. A lot of the knowledge needed by the community will be found and taken (mined) from the oral information system.

Useful communication strategies:

a) *Reading clubs*: Reading clubs help the semi-literate people increase and strengthen their reading skills. They will read newspapers, literacy primers, and novels. The CIRC may invite a speaker to talk about a topic that the club members have read about. In this way, club members can share and contribute their own thinking on the topic.

b) *Radio and audio-cassette listening forums:* The CIRC will organise listening forums around radio programmes with interesting development content. Community radio is particularly useful for this purpose because its programmes have a lot of local content. The listening forums can also share their knowledge by producing their own programmes through the community radio. For example, health, agriculture extension programmes, and drama with community development themes are good topics. After the radio programme is finished, the participants can discuss the issues and develop action plans, whenever possible.

c) *Video viewing*: Video viewing can provide information access to all community members, including the group of semi-literate people. Video shows on development and entertainment themes, followed by discussions, will help raise awareness of development issues in the community.

d) *Internet services*: Community members can access vast quantities of information through the Internet. To use this tool, the community members need to become computer literate, so that they can search for the information they need without major difficulties. An information worker can do the Internet search for those who are not computer literate.

10.6.1.2. Women Members

Women play multiple roles in many societies. As a result, they find it difficult, as a group, to participate fully in information sharing activities. Most women work on the farms with men. When they return from farming, women have to prepare food for the family, and quite often fetch water and firewood. They look after young children and do other household chores. These multiple social roles leave women with little time to participate in the structured information and knowledge exchange activities of a CIRC.

In some cases, women have additional problems because their activities outside the household are limited by husbands and by age-old customs. Women and girls may have to ask for permission to leave their own compound. It is assumed that 'a good woman does not wander around aimlessly in public'. In some places, young unmarried women walking to an information centre alone risk abduction, rape, and other forms of harassment by men in the community.

Useful communication strategies:

a) Finding space and time, when the workload of women allows them to participate in the activities of the information centre. Christian women may have some free time on Sundays; Moslem women on Fridays.

b) Groups of women may form networks and clubs, so that they can hold meetings. During the meetings, they will read useful materials together and hold discussions. On such occasions, the CIRC can be closed to other members of the community to ensure there is adequate space for the women. Such social networks provide solidarity to individuals. The networks empower them to use some of the services of the information centre without breaking any social codes.

c) Women's groups can meet in the house of one of their members on a rotational basis to hold discussions, watch a video or listen to a radio programme. In this way, they participate in the activities of the CIRC. Successful women from other parts of the country can also be invited to tell their stories on how to set up networks. These stories inspire other women and give them ideas on how to uplift themselves.

10.6.1.3. Young Community Members

Young people between the ages of 13 and 25 years are in a difficult position. They are neither children nor full adults. In most cultures, the young people do not get equal opportunities (occasions) to express their views or to participate fully in development activities, on their own terms.

With the outbreak of HIV/AIDS, Sexually Transmitted Diseases (STDs), and early pregnancies, this group is on the front line of many of the development issues in the community. The young people do not have many opportunities (occasions) to express their point of view towards finding solutions to problems that face them and their community. Another serious issue is the cultural breakdown between generations in most communities. As a result of the modernisation model of development, urbanisation, and the effect of Western-oriented mass media, many young people are estranged from their own culture. They try hard to copy various forms of Western culture, but without success.

Useful communication strategies:

a) This group has a great need for intelligent information on the basics of human behaviour, especially sexual behaviour. Information on sexual and reproductive health matters is crucial for young people, if they are to avoid the problems of Sexually Transmitted Diseases (STDs) and early pregnancy.

b) Introducing young people to their own cultural heritage through folklore, songs, poetry, handicrafts, traditional agricultural and health practices helps to ensure that they do not grow up in a cultural void. All these elements need to be critically examined to decide if they are suitable for today's social situation. Culture is living. It changes because culture is part of being human and social. Culture must evolve (change) and address new situations. Cultural knowledge, like all forms of knowledge, cannot be allowed to be static (unchanging) or it will wither and die.

c) Many young people will still be students, continuing their education.

They need educational materials of all types, as well as a quiet place to study, so they can do their schoolwork successfully. It is difficult to find space and the right environment at home, because the house is crowded and there is no study area.

References

Adam, Lishan, "An Information-Driven Community Paradigm and an Organic Growth", *Towards Adoption of Information and Communication Technologies: the Case of Illubabor Community Libraries in Ethiopia,* Addis Ababa, 2002.

Mchombu, Kingo J., *Information Needs and Seeking Patterns for Rural Peoples Development in Africa,* Gaborone, Botswana: (Print and Publishing Co.), 1993.

Mchombu, Kingo, *Sharing Knowledge for Community Development and Transformation: A Handbook,* Oxfam - HOACBP - CIDA, 2004.

O'siochru, Seán, "Community ownership of ICTs: New possibilities for poor communities", en *WSIS Papers,* 2005.

Praverand, Pierre, "Knowledge is Power" in *International Development Review,* v. 22, no.1, 1980.

Robinson S., Scott, *Rethinking Telecentres in the Second World: Knowledge demands,* remittance flows and microbanks, Ciudad de México, 2000.

11

Agricultural Education and Training for Rural Development

Due to increasing urbanisation, fed by out-migration from rural areas, governments often give priority to urban needs for health, education and social services at the expense of rural areas and the agricultural sector. Such action leads to even greater impoverishment in rural areas and leads to higher levels of migration. Without comprehensive rural development policies, rural populations are further marginalised by a more organised urban sector with a greater political voice.

Agricultural institutions are becoming increasingly isolated from the mainstream of national development and need to play a more dynamic role in rural development issues through better links with government and with other institutions. Countries in transition towards an industry-based economy, such as China and Korea, mentioned social problems arising from the rejection of the rural/agricultural way of life by educated young people.

In addition to problems of recruiting students into programmes of agricultural study, the marginalisation of the rural world is demonstrated by changes in urban/rural relationships. The perceptions that urban people have of agriculture and rural activities are often divorced from reality. In general, urban populations view rural areas as suppliers of food and primary products to meet their consumption needs.

In response to these problems, some universities are adjusting their training objectives, making them more relevant to the current needs of agriculture and rural people. For example, they now are including in their programmes subjects such as marketing, biotechnology, computerisation, development communication systems, and non-agricultural rural land use.

11.1. Improving Agricultural Education System

In many developing countries, rural young people find difficulty in obtaining a basic education of the same quality as urban youth, and hence the difficulty in gaining entrance to higher education institutions. This situation is unlikely to change as long as entrance to these institutions is based solely on academic qualifications which place rural young people in direct competition with better schooled urban youth. The result is a significant waste of human resources, since rural youth possess unique aptitudes and qualities for understanding of and work in the rural sector. The rural background make them well suited for professional and technical work in agriculture. Rural young men and women are a human resource which is not developed to its fullest potential.

Rural young women have a particular disadvantage in gaining access to agricultural education and training. Even when they receive a good basic education, they have less access to the secondary and higher education levels. In some cultures, increased numbers of females with agricultural skills are needed since only female extension agents are allowed to work directly with women farmers.

The low standards of general education in rural areas of developing countries make it difficult for rural young men and women to obtain the entry level qualifications for access to agricultural education, particularly at the higher levels. Ways to improve access by rural youth include short courses to upgrade students to the required standards, the provision of continuing education and specific "bridges" between the various levels of education.

11.1.1. Concept of Rural Universities

The original concept of rural universities encompassed the education which would be in the context of rural growth, culture and development, not confined to crop production alone. However, the circumstances during the postindependent period resulted in emphasis on crops or more specifically grain production for meeting the food grain demand in the country and to avoid import of food grains. Consequently, the emphasis on resource management of natural, human and monetary inputs was not adequately placed. This possibly also was the legacy of preindependent India.

One of the major achievements of agriculture management systems was to recognise the need of integration of research, education and extension. All agricultural universities have separate Departments of Agriculture Extension, which not only teach the principles of extension but in fact practice it also. They have developed various techniques of demonstration and communication. However, in all the states, Departments of Agriculture exist and are responsible for the extension services in the concerned state.

The agricultural technology is based on the following biophysical factors:

- Understanding of location-specific climate/weather.
- Soil characteristics, including its physical, chemical and biological properties.
- Appropriate soil treatment.
- Assessment of suitability of crops for a crop season.
- Knowledge and assessment of different diseases, insect pests, nematodes and weeds and their potential for competition with different crops.
- Availability and arrangement of the various inputs, crops varieties with alternative choices, water, fertilisers, pesticides, energy source and labour.
- Facility for availability of seed material and its testing or other plant material.
- Time management for different operations for the success of agricultural production.

All the above aspects must be integrated and implemented. This amounts to saying that an extension scientist, besides having the knowledge and means of communication, should be aware or be supported by specialist in the above areas. The following are the few common constraints:

- Appropriate knowledge of nutrients of the soil, though farmers often have a good idea about their soil.

- Non-availability of the right seed of a recommended variety and seed quality.
- Supply of poor or adulterated quality of fertiliser and chemicals.
- Lack of availability of water or the source of energy at appropriate time.
- Pest management operations in early stages to control epidemic.
- Repair of agricultural implements.

11.2. Agriculture Education and Agricultural Extension Programmes

Agriculture education and agricultural extension programmes, improve the traditional skills of farmers and to impart new appropriate skills. Agricultural trends are changing everyday with the development of new techniques. To make the best of emerging technologies, it is vital that agriculturalists receive continuous education and training. This training is provided on topics such as pesticide management, use of better seeds, irrigation and use of fertilisers among many others. Equally important is the process of agricultural research and development to create cheaper and better farm practices. The Central and State Governments have made major contributions in this area.

11.2.1. Agricultural Extension Programmes

It is important to disseminate information about new technologies so that the farmer is able to make use of the latest agricultural developments. There also exists a gap between research findings and the needs of farmers. For technology to be successful, it is important that it should serve a useful purpose to the end user. The institution that bridges the gap between farmers and agricultural research scientists is the Agricultural Extension Service. This service works through an Agricultural Research System in the States.

The main objective of Agriculture Extension Services or AES's is to transmit latest technical know-how to farmers. Besides this, the AESs also focuses on enhancing farmers' knowledge about crop techniques and helping them to increase productivity. This is done through training courses, farm visits, on farm trials, kisan melas, kisan clubs, advisory bulletins and the like.

The National Institute of Agricultural Extension Management is an apex national institute set under the Ministry of Agriculture, Government of India. It assists the State Governments, the Government of India and other public sector organisations in effective management of their agricultural extension and other agricultural management systems.

11.2.2. Farmers Training

Farmers' training is provided at the local level through Krishi Vigyan Kendras, vocational agricultural schools and field demonstrations. These training classes may be conducted on specific topics like the use of urea or vast topics like packages of practice. The new information that farmers gain through these training sessions makes their daily farming activities much easier. It also leads to an increase in productivity and bigger profits in the long run.

11.2.3. State Agricultural Universities

The State Agricultural Universities are major partners in the growth and development of agricultural research and education under the national agricultural research system. Currently, there are 41 State Agricultural Universities in India. These agricultural universities are responsible for research, training and dissemination of agriculture related information in the State. They generate new technologies to increase production, provide degree and certificate programmes in agriculture and help in the transfer of technology by participating in farmer training classes organised by local agricultural bodies.

The State Agricultural Universities carry out research programmes to tackle location specific problems of different agro-climatic zones. The research programmes and activities are constantly and critically reviewed and the research activities are mainly focused on thrust areas identified. Research, to constantly improve and generate technologies for increasing production in agriculture, animal husbandry, home science and allied sectors is one of the major mandates of these universities.

11.2.3.1. Krishi Darshan

Krishi Darshan is an agriculture related television programme that is broadcast by the government on its exclusive terrestrial television network - Doordarshan. It is a half hour programme that is run five days a week at 6.30 pm. The content is created in collaboration with the Ministry of Agriculture, Government of India, under the Mass Media Support to Agriculture Extension Scheme. Krishi Darshan includes features, documentaries, success stories of farmers, research inputs, quizzes, crop seminars and a live phone in programme. It covers various aspects of agriculture and related activities like horticulture, animal husbandry, dairy and rural life.

11.2.3.2. ATMA Centres

The Agricultural Technology Management Agency (ATMA) is a society of key stakeholders who carry out agricultural activities for sustainable agricultural growth of a district. It involves a combination of research and extension activities, so that new agricultural technologies are distributed over a district. This allows it to receive and spend project finances, enter into contracts and maintain revolving accounts. These revolving accounts are utilised for collecting fees and thereby recovering operating costs.

ATMA Centres have links with local line departments, research organisations, non-governmental organisations and agencies associated with agricultural development in the district. Research and Extension units within the project districts, Krishi Vigyan Kendras, and the departments of agriculture, animal husbandry, horticulture and fisheries are constituent members of ATMA. Programmes and procedures that concern district research and extension activities are determined by the governing board of ATMA centres and implemented by its management committee

11.2.3.3. Krishi Vigyan Kendras

Krishi Vigyan Kendras (KVKs) are a project of the Indian Council of Agricultural Research for the testing and transfer of agricultural technologies. These organisations are meant to bridge the gap between production and productivity and to increase self-employment opportunities among the farming community. The training offered at these centres follows the principles of "learning by doing" and "seeing is believing". KVK's offer skill and knowledge oriented training in multidisciplinary areas such as –

- Crop production
- Plant protection
- Horticulture
- Animal sciences
- Fisheries
- Home science
- Agricultural extension.

11.2.4. ICAR Research Centres

The Indian Council of Agricultural Research (ICAR) is a storehouse of agricultural information. It also offers consultancy services in agriculture, horticulture, animal sciences, fisheries, resource management, agricultural engineering, agricultural education, agricultural extension, home science and agricultural communication. The co-ordination of agricultural research and development programmes comes under its purview. ICAR is also responsible for generating contacts with related organisations in the national and international arena to better the standard of life of agriculturalists.

The ICAR after reorganisation became responsible for agriculture research in the country. The reorganisation did not specifically make ICAR responsible for education for agriculture but creation of the position of the Deputy Director-General (Education) implicitly meant some role of ICAR in agriculture education. This was further formalised when a Department of Agriculture Research and Education (DARE) was created. However, the fact remains that agricultural universities are established under the UGC Act. Therefore, ICAR plays no role in establishment of agricultural universities, and yet a relationship between ICAR and agricultural universities has been established. This relationship is not entirely based on any major financial support to agricultural universities by ICAR.

ICAR has established a number of research centres to meet the agricultural research and education needs of the country. It actively pursues human resource development through the setting up of agricultural universities in different parts of the country. The Technology Intervention Programmes are also an integral part of ICAR's agenda. These programmes help establish Krishi Vigyan Kendras (KVKs) which are responsible for training, research and demonstration of new farming technologies at the local level.

References

Lindsay Falvey, *Food Environment Education: Agricultural Education in Natural Resource Management*, 1966.

Newcomb L. H., and others, *Methods of Teaching Agriculture by Interstate*, 1986.

Randhawa, M. S., *A History of Agriculture in India*, 1979.

Subramaniam, C., in *Wheat Revolution* (ed. Swaminathan, M. S.), 1993.

Bibliography

Abu-Ghaida, D. and S. Klasen, "The Costs of Missing the Millennium Development Goal on Gender Equity," *World Development*, Vol. 32, No. 7., Elsevier: Great Britain: 2004.

Acker, D. (Ed.), "Leadership for higher education in agriculture", *Proceedings of the inaugural conference of the Global Consortium of Higher Education and Research for Agriculture*, Ames, Iowa: Iowa State University, 1999.

Ahmed, M.; Coombs, P.H., *Education for rural development—case studies for planners*, New York: Praeger Publishers, 1975.

Anderlini, S.N., *Women at the Peace Table: Making a Difference*, UNIFEM: New York: 2000.

Bajpai, Piyush and Mayank Singh, "The Death of Indian Languages on the Internet", *The Case of Hindi, background paper, Indicus Analytics*, New Delhi, 2005.

Bawden, R., "Agricultural education and training: future perspectives", *Paper prepared for the Agricultural Knowledge and Information Systems (AKIS) thematic team in the Rural Family of the World Bank*, 1998.

Behrman J., A. Foster, M. Rosenzweig and P.Vashishthe, "Women's Schooling, Home Teaching, and Economic Growth," *Journal of Political Economy*, Vol.107, No.4, 1999.

Behrman, Jere R. and James C. Knowles, "Household Income and Child Schooling in Vietnam" *World Bank Economic Review*, 1999.

Bennell, P., "Learning to change: skills development among the economically vulnerable and socially excluded in developing countries", In: *Employment and Training Papers*, Geneva: ILO, 1999.

Berstecher, D., *Education and rural development: issues for planning and research*, Paris: IIEP-UNESCO, 1985.

Bhatnagar, Subhash and Robert Schware, *Information and Communication Technology in Development: Cases from India*, New Delhi: Sage Publications, 2000.

Brock, C. and Cammish, N.K., "Factors affecting female participation in education in seven developing countries," *DIFID Education*, London: DIFID, Serial No. 9, 1997.

Brown II, C. (Ed.), "Organization and governance in higher education (Fifth edition)", *ASHE Reader Series*, Boston: Pearson Custom Publishing, 2000.

Bude, U. (Ed.), *Culture and environment in primary education*, Bonn: DSE, ZED, 1993.

Cammish, N. and Brock, C., "Girls, Schools and Limits to Change", *ID21 Society and Economy*, 4 March 1999.

CERID, "Promotion of Girls' Education", *Through Recruitment and Training of Female Teachers in Nepal: A country case study*, Kathmandu: Center for Educational Research, Innovation and Development, 1996.

Coombs, P.H.; Manzoor, A., *Attacking rural poverty: how nonformal education can help*, Baltimore, MD: Johns Hopkins University Press, 1974.

Datt, G. and M. Ravallion, "Farm Productivity and Rural Poverty In India", *Journal of Development Studies*, vol.34, no.4, 1998.

_______________ , "How Important to India's Poor is the Sectoral Composition of Economic Growth?' *The World Bank Economic Review*, vol.10, no.1, 1996.

Epstein, Joyce L.; Lucretia Coates; Karen Clark Salinas; Mavis G. Sanders; and Beth S. Simon, "School, Family, and Community Partnerships: Your Handbook for Action", 1997.

FAO, *Training for agriculture and rural development 1995-96*, Rome: FAO, 1996.

_______________ , *Report of the expert consultation on strategy options for higher education in agriculture*, Rome, Italy, Rome: FAO, 16-20 December 1991.

Frost, G., "Learning the value of girls education, Oxfam. Sa Pa, Viet Nam, 1999.

Gaiha, R. & Kulkarni, V., "Is growth central to poverty alleviation in India?", *Journal of International Affairs*, 1998.

Gaiha, R., "Poverty alleviation programs in rural India: an assessment", *Development and Change*, 1991.

Gaynor, Cathy, *Decentralisation of Education: Teacher Management*, Washington, DC: World Bank, 1998.

Goldring, E. B., "Community and Parents' Participation in Curriculum Decisions", In *The International Encyclopedia of Education*, Second Edition Volume 2, 1994.

Govinda, R; Varghese, N.V., *Quality of primary schooling in India: a case study of Madhya Pradesh,* Paris: IIEP-UNESCO, 1993.

Heneveld, Ward and Helen Craig, "Schools Count: World Bank Project Designs and the Quality of Primary Education in Sub-Saharan Africa", Washington, DC: The World Bank, 1996.

Janke, C., *Food and Education: background considerations for policy and programming,* Catholic Relief Services, 2001.

Khan Mahmood, H., *Rural poverty in developing countries, implications for public policy.* Washington DC: International Monetary Fund, 2001.

Kunkel, H.O.; Maw, L.; Skaggs, C.L., (Eds), *Revolutionizing higher education in agriculture, framework for change,* Ames, IA: Iowa State University Press, 1996.

Liu, Y.; Jingzun, Z., "The reform of higher agricultural education institutions in China", *Case study prepared for IIEP,* 2002.

Lovell, Catherine H., *Breaking the Cycle of Poverty: The BRAC Strategy,* West Hartford, Connecticut: Kumarian Press, Inc., 1992.

Maimbolwa-Sinyangwe, I. M. and B.Y. Chilangwa, "Learning from Inside the Classroom: A research report", UNICEF/Ministry of Education, Zambia, December 1995.

Mchombu, Kingo, *Sharing Knowledge for Community Development and Transformation: A Handbook,* Oxfam - HOACBP - CIDA, 2004.

Melnychuk, D., *The reform of higher agricultural education institutions in Ukraine,* National Agricultural University of Ukraine, 2002.

Moulton, J., *Improving education in rural areas: guidance for rural development specialists* (draft), Washington DC: World Bank, 2001.

Narayan-Parker, Deepa, *Designing community based development,* Washington, DC: The World Bank, 1995.

Nilay M.Yajnik, "The potential of the Advanced Internet Project for India", *proceedings of the Annual Conference of the Computer Society of India,* Chennai, India, September 2000.

O'siochru, Seán, "Community ownership of ICTs: New possibilities for poor communities", en *WSIS Papers,* 2005.

OECD (Organisation for Economic Co-operation and Development), *Parents as Partners in Schooling,* Paris: OECD, Center for Educational Research and Innovation, 1997.

Ravallion, M. and G. Datt, "Farm Productivity and Rural Poverty in India", *Journal of Development Studies,* vol.34, no.4, 1998.

Reddy, B.S., *Education and rural development in rural India,* Paris: IIEP-UNESCO, 2001.

Riedmiller, S., "Primary school agriculture—What can it realistically achieve?" In: *Entwicklung Landlicher Raum* (3), 1994..

Stiglitz, J., *Globalization and its discontents,* New York: Norton, 2002.

Szekely, C., "Effects of structural and functional change in agriculture on the development of higher agricultural education in Europe", *Paper presented at the 4th European Conference on Higher agricultural education,* Moscow, 1998.

Taylor, P.; Mulhall, A., *Contextualizing teaching and learning in rural primary schools: using agricultural experience,* Vol. I. London: DFID, 1997.

Tuan, Y., "Children and the natural environment", In: Altman, I. and Wohlwill, J.F., (Eds), *Children and the Environment.* New York: Plenium Press, 1978.

UN Millennium Project, Task Force on Education and Gender Equality, *Toward Universal Primary Education: Investments, Incentives, and Institutions,* Earthscan: London/Sterling,VA: 2005.

UNESCO, *EFA Global Monitoring Report 2003-04, Gender and Education for All:The Leap to Equality,* Paris: 2003.

_______________, *Gender and Education for All: The Leap to Equality: Summary Report,* Paris: 2003.

_______________, *Women and Girls: Education, Not Discrimination,* New York: 2000.

United Nations Children's Fund, *The State of the World's Children 2003,* UNICEF, New York, 2002.

Van Lierop, P., "Ecology education in primary schools", In: *ILEIA Newsletter,* 1997.

World Bank, *Effective schooling in rural communities. Key topics,* Washington DC: World Bank, 2000.

_______________, *India—Poverty Reduction: Progress and Challenges,* Washington, D.C.World Bank: World Development Report, 2000.

World Food Programme, *School feeding works for girls' education,* Rome: WFP, 2001.

Index